WILD CATS

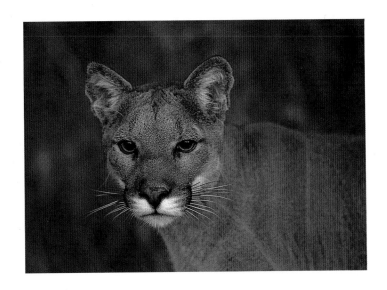

WILD CATS
LYNX ▪ BOBCATS ▪ MOUNTAIN LIONS

C A N D A C E   S A V A G E

Sierra Club Books
San Francisco

The author gratefully acknowledges the assistance of Daryll Hebert of Alberta Pacific Forest Industries, Paul Galbraith of Parks Canada, Martin Jalkotzy and Ian Ross of the Alberta Cougar Project, Arlen Todd of Alberta Forestry Lands and Wildlife, and John Seidensticker of the Smithsonian Institution, all of whom reviewed the manuscript for this book and offered expert advice.

Originally published in Canada by Greystone Books, Douglas & McIntyre, 1615 Venables Street, Vancouver, British Columbia V5L 2H1

Library of Congress Cataloging-in-Publication Data

Savage, Candace Sherk, 1949–
    Wild cats / Candace Savage
       p.   cm.
    ISBN 0-87156-424-6
    1.Felidae—North America.   I. Title.
QL737.C23S285 1993
599.74'428'097—dc20   93-2821
                                     CIP

Production by Terri Wershler
Cover design by Rose Cowles
Book design by Rose Cowles
Title page photograph: Mountain lion
    by Victoria Hurst
Printed and bound in Singapore

10 9 8 7 6 5 4 3 2

CONTENTS

INTRODUCTION 1

LYNX AND BOBCATS 5

MOUNTAIN LIONS 63

ABUNDANT LIFE 119

REFERENCES 130

INDEX 135

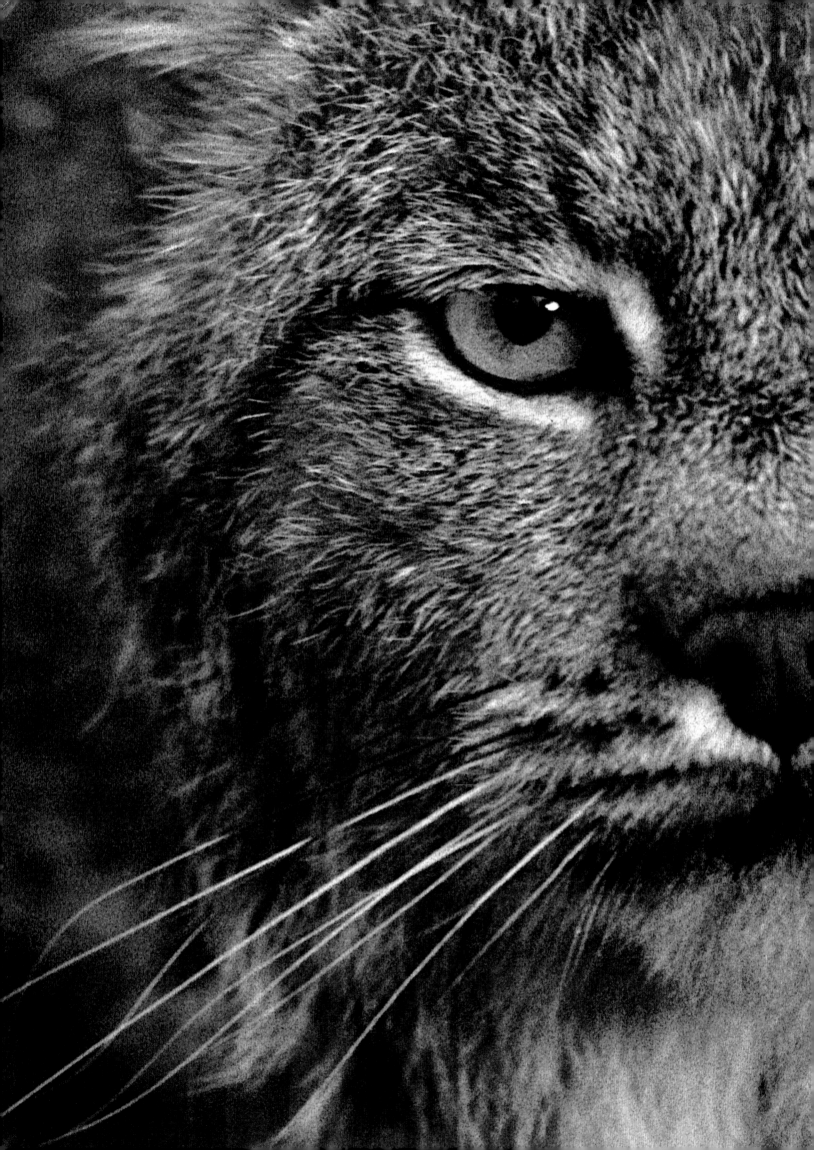

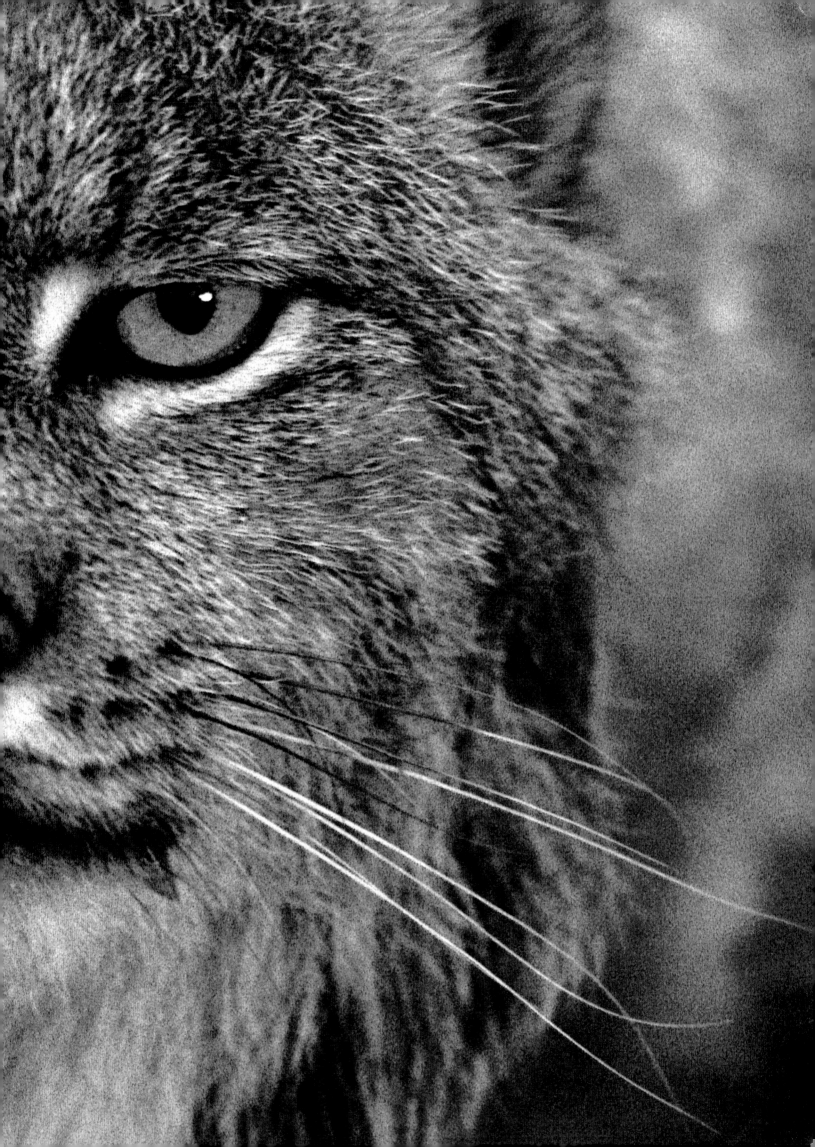

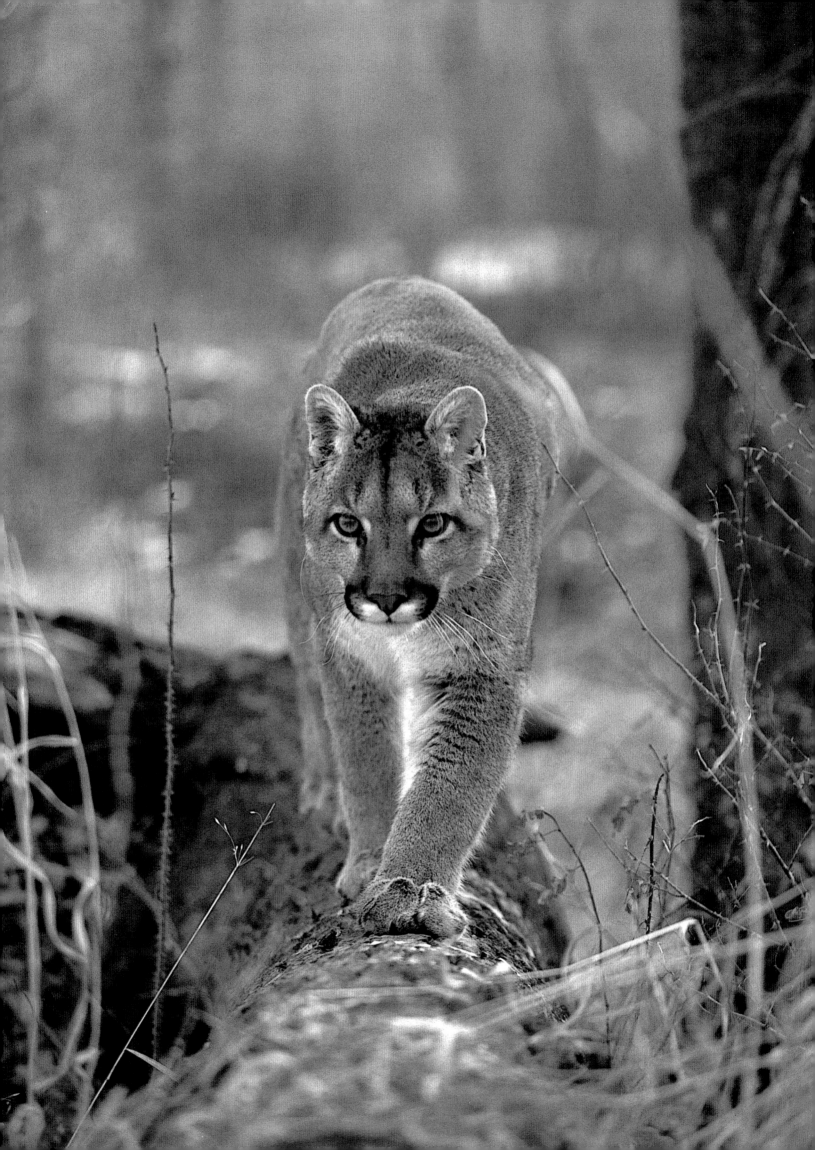

INTRODUCTION

When we hear the words "wild cats," our minds fill with images of exotic beasts in faraway places. A pride of lions sprawled in the dusty heat of the African plains. A tiger rippling through the damp green shade of a tropical rainforest. But there are other wild cats that live much closer to home and that, surprisingly, are not so widely known. This book offers an intimate look at three of our feline neighbours—the lynx, the bobcat and the mountain lion.

If you put a house cat in a box and tell it to stay put, you can be reasonably sure that it will leap out within two minutes. Lynx, bobcats and mountain lions are, if anything, less biddable. They even resist being put into intellectual boxes, such as classification systems. Taxonomists still haven't been able to determine if there are one or three species of lynx, or if lynx and bobcats belong to the same genus as mountain lions or ought to have their own grouping. Nor are the cats easier to pin down by geography. Although the ranges of the three species overlap in North America, lynx and mountain lions spill off the continent in different directions — lynx across Eurasia and mountain lions to the tip of South America.

For the sake of simplicity, this book focusses on the cats of North America, Europe and Asia, in the North Temperate Zone. More specifically, it concentrates on the temperate forest, a wide belt of woodlands that arises first as stunted

Mountain lion. *Denver Bryan*

brush on the edge of the barrengrounds. Sweeping southward, this growth coalesces to form a dense cloak of conifers flung around the shoulders of the northern continents. At its southern margin, the coniferous fabric becomes interwoven with stands of deciduous growth and then gradually unravels into the leafy dappled woodlands of southern Canada, the United States and southern Eurasia. These sheltered lands constitute critical habitat for all three species of cats: virtually all lynx, most bobcats and many mountain lions live in and around the temperate forest.

But northern forests do more than offer living space to wild cats. They also provide raw materials to some of the most highly industrialized countries on Earth and, consequently, number amongst the most altered and exploited of all ecosystems. Western Europe, now a crazy-quilt patchwork of cities and croplands, was once almost completely forested. (Small wonder that France, western Germany, the Netherlands and Portugal currently have more than 40 per cent of their mammals on the "threatened" list.) According to a recent audit, the forests of Russia, which encompass almost one-fifth of the world's woodlands, have suffered from decades of overharvest. In the United States, the area devoted to forest declines slightly each year, a pattern that is reiterated in Canadian statistics. Although we have no rigorous way to assess the biological quality of the forests that remain, their health as living communities is almost certainly worsening.

This deterioration is often referred to as "loss of habitat," but it might more usefully be described as the destruction of life-support systems. Wild cats and other predators may seem high and mighty ("the king of the beasts") but, like us, they are profoundly dependent. They are dependent on their prey; they are dependent on the grass, leaves, bark and twigs that their prey eat. They are dependent on the organisms in the forest soil that feed the plants that feed the prey, etc. When people go forth with plows, bulldozers and chainsaws, we often unwittingly break these life-giving connections. Using paper or wood from a ruined forest can kill just as surely as if we'd gone out with guns. Yet because there are no dead bodies to count, we may not sense what we have done.

Overall, wild cats are in crisis. Of the roughly three dozen species worldwide, "almost all are declining seriously in numbers because of human impact," according to experts with the World Conservation Union. "Every indicator suggests that declines are accelerating and have reached, in some cases, a critical stage."

Fortunately, lynx, bobcats and mountain lions are among the few species to escape this frightening prognosis. Although lynx and mountain lions have suffered grave losses in the past, neither they nor bobcats are in any immediate danger of extinction. But this does not mean that we can rest easy about their status. For one thing, they are cats and are therefore especially susceptible to the harmful effects of industrial society, including our assault on the natural communities in which they participate. For another, all three species are currently killed for profit, whether to obtain furs, to protect livestock or for entertainment. While this does not necessarily spell disaster, we know from tragic experience that the commercial exploitation of wild cats is perilous and can easily lead to their depletion, or extinction. It has happened to snow leopards, tigers, ocelots; it could happen again.

But the most important reason for turning our attention to mountain lions, bobcats and lynx is precisely because they are not endangered. While it makes us feel saintly to run around "saving" plants and animals from doom (a doom that we have usually caused in the first place), it is wasteful of time, altruism and money. How much wiser it would be for us to devote ourselves to maintaining healthy populations and viable natural communities, where we still have a chance. Our first priority should always be to safeguard abundance.

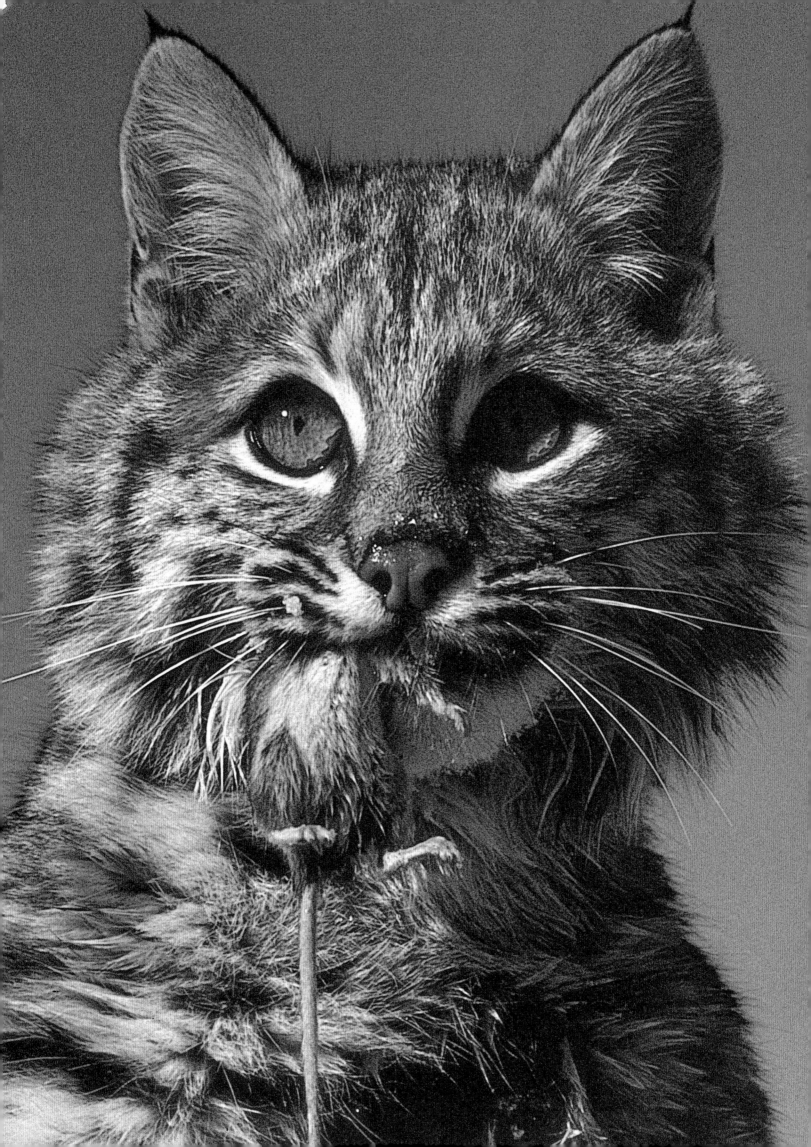

LYNX AND BOBCATS

THE WORD "RESPECT," IN ITS ROOT SENSE,
MEANS "TO LOOK AGAIN."
WHEN WE LOOK AGAIN AT THE FOREST,
WE MAY SEE CATS LOOKING BACK.

Twenty years have passed, but I have never forgotten the day I saw the lynx. I was hiking along the edge of a wooded ravine, came around a corner, and there it stood: a gangly cat, about thigh-high, with a broad ruffed face, yellow eyes and feathery tufts on its ears. We stared at each other. A heartbeat, two. Then, silently, the cat turned away and melted into the bush.

"Wood ghosts," people used to call them, and with good reason. Cats, by their deepest nature, are elusive. To understand why, just watch Puss in the vegetable patch. When a bird flutters down from the trees, she crouches low and shields herself behind a screen of leaves. Instead of walking, her supple body flows forward, as if her bones and muscles have changed to a slow liquid. Her footfall is silent. A few seconds away from her prey, she stops, gathers her legs underneath her and fidgets her hind end. On the other side of the bean row, the bird goes on feeding. And then the cat is on it in a single well-aimed leap. Her soft paws are suddenly armed with claws, and her strong jaws are biting.

With variations of prey and place, this is the way most wild cats make their living. They are solitary hunters that take their prey unawares, pouncing out of nowhere to kill with a precisely placed bite to the neck. Accordingly, their jaws are short for extra power (no long dog snout for them), their eye teeth (the poorly named "canines") are exceptionally

Bobcat with mouse. *Erwin & Peggy Bauer*

5

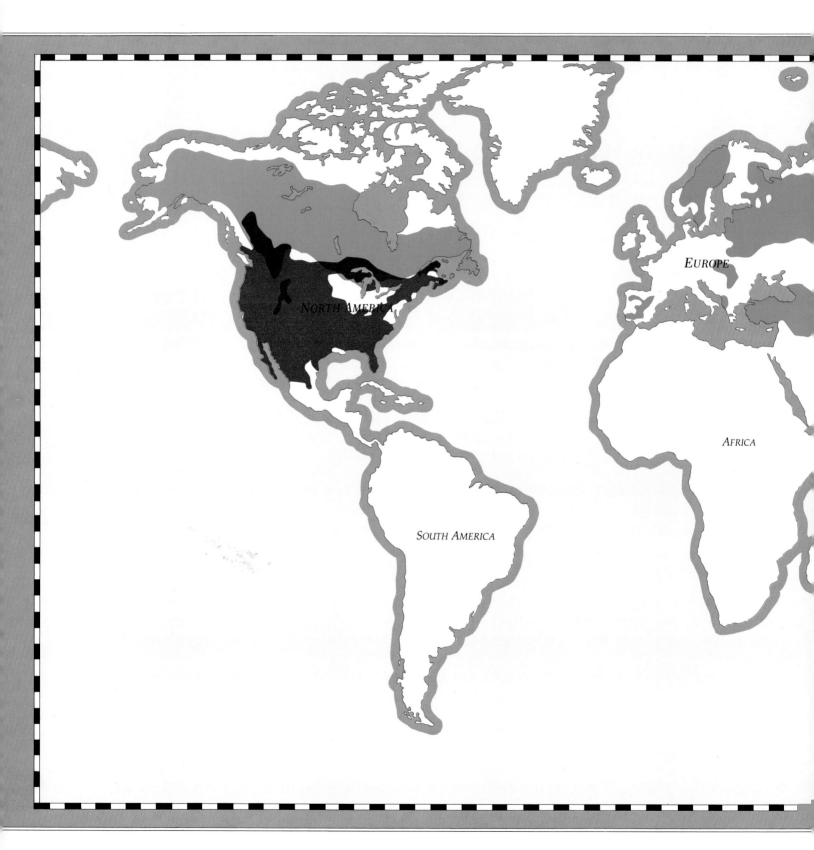

NORTH AMERICA

SOUTH AMERICA

EUROPE

AFRICA

Lynx distribution is based on a map in "Felix lynx," *Mammalian Species* 269 by Renn Tumlinson, 1987. Bobcat distribution comes from *A Critical and Annotated Bibliography of Literature on the Bobcat* by Eric M. Anderson, 1987.

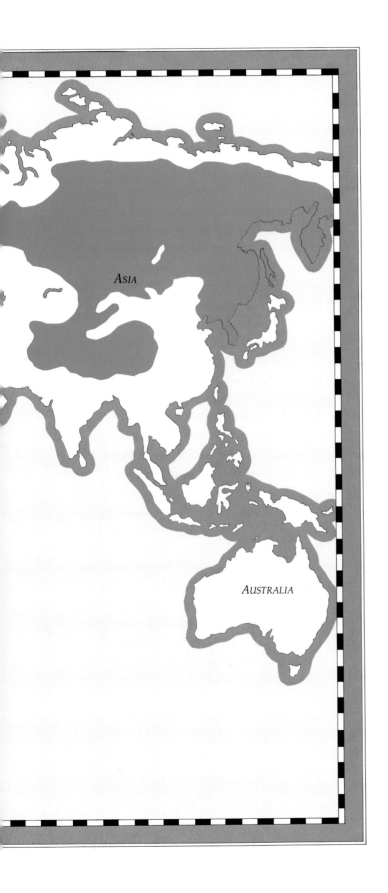

PRESENT DISTRIBUTION OF THE LYNX AND THE BOBCAT

Lynx formerly ranged throughout Europe, from Scandinavia east to Siberia and south to the Caucasus Mountains. The species' range has diminished during the last 2,000 years because of human hunting and land use. The range of the bobcat has been largely unchanged during this period.

LYNX

BOBCATS

long and pointed, and their claws can be retracted to keep them sharp as pins. Their graceful, athletic bodies have been perfected over millions of years for stealth and explosive, last-minute surprise.

But these impressive adaptations are also limiting. A skeleton that has been designed for pouncing is not suited for running long distances. And a nature that is tuned to solitude cannot regularly resort to co-operative hunting. If a cat is clumsy and alarms its prey, its meal will likely sprint off, and it will seldom have the benefit of a hunting partner to make good on the missed opportunity. For a cat, a lost chance usually translates directly to an empty belly. Thus, the basic precepts of cathood are clear. Stay hidden and you eat; be conspicuous and you starve. Lynx and bobcats stay hidden.

So when I set out to look for lynx again, I knew the chance of success wasn't good. To improve the odds, I enlisted the help of Paul Galbraith, an ecologist and chief warden of Prince Albert National Park in north-central Saskatchewan, Canada—"on the southern edge," the brochures say, "of the great northern forest." A good-humoured man with mild blue eyes, Paul has spent most of his life in the north woods and has travelled it on foot, in canoes and by dogsled and snow-machine. On this day in late winter, he has agreed to take me skiing into lynx country. From the first moment, it is clear that he has something important to say, not just about lynx but about the forest they inhabit.

"There's so much of this we don't *sense*," he says as we snap our feet into our skis. "So much of the life of the forest that we don't even notice."

I squint into the open woods, hoping to see what I've missed. Fringing the edge of the trail are clusters of young spruce, with delicate, frondlike branches that screen the deeper woods. Behind them, as if standing guard, are ranks of older trees with coarse drooping branches and grey reptilian skin. Among them and startling white, the long naked trunks of poplars reach towards the light. Here and there the trees make room for ponds and shrubby breaks.

Stride, glide, stride, glide into the forest. For a long while we follow the deep doggy tracks of a wolf—one of about two dozen meat-eating species in the area. Paul rattles off the names of the major carnivores of the north woods, a list that includes martens, fishers, otters, minks, weasels, skunks, wolverines, wolves, coyotes, foxes, owls, eagles, hawks and, of course, lynx. All these predators compete for the same limited forest resource, the flesh of plant-eating animals. How do they all manage to make a living? More specifically, with all that competition, how do lynx manage, year in, year out, to get enough to eat?

For lynx, Paul explains, part of the answer lies in their feline ancestry, which has given them the gifts of precision and secrecy. They can take advantage of hunting opportunities that are not available to most other predators. In addition, they are specially adapted to life in a particular kind of forest. "We'll come to it just ahead—true boreal forest. Excellent lynx habitat."

We let the bright slash of the cutline lead us farther north. Sure enough, the forest is different here. No more poplars, only spruce, and the air is spiced and cool. On both sides of the trail the trees rise like a wall. When I peer in among them, my eyes lose their way in a prickly darkness. A few minutes farther along the trail, the gloom gives way to an open lakeshore. This varied landscape—dense conifers (for denning and shelter) interrupted by burned areas or brushy breaks (for hunting)—is the lynx's home.

In the winter the northern forest is deep-snow country, and more than most other predators, lynx are adapted to meet this difficulty. Their legs are extra long to help them through the drifts, and their feet are broad and padded with hair to serve as snowshoes. Accordingly, their tracks are surprisingly large—wider than an adult's hand—and look smudged or blurred because they're so heavily furred. Since their claws are retractable, the tips don't show in the snow. Paul has often seen tracks on precisely this stretch of the trail.

It is exhilarating to think that there are lynx nearby. In my mind's eye I see them padding silently along fallen logs; slinking, bellies to the ground, through the willows. Some are bedded under trees and lie dozing, licking their toes. One sits on its haunches in a small clearing and calmly watches us ski past. I scan the forest expectantly, allowing myself to half believe I'll catch a lynx looking back.

We ski for the rest of the morning, stop for lunch beside a frozen pond and ski out again. We do not see a lynx, of course, not so much as a track. A typical lynx-watching trip. But I know from my high spirits that this failure is a success. I've had a chance to "sense" lynx in the complexity of their forest.

Unhappily, this experience would not have been possible in large parts of the cats' natural range. Even though lynx are hard to observe, they are easy to kill. A shiny piece of paper or an interesting scent will lure them into a trap. A bawling dog sends them up a tree, where they make ready targets. Predictably, the effects of this

vulnerability have sometimes been calamitous. Once resident across Eurasia, the lynx is now extinct, or severely endangered, in all of central Europe. In Italy, the species was destroyed through what scientists now term a "slaughter," carried out to prevent "alleged damages" to small livestock. In recent years, when a few cats slipped back into the area from a reintroduced population in nearby Switzerland, they were often met with the same vengeance.

In the Vosges mountains of northeastern France, the primary causes of the lynx's extirpation appear to have been sport hunting and, more particularly, the centuries-old fur business. As far back as the Middle Ages, a high price was placed on lynx pelts, which were valued on a par with leopard skins brought in by spice merchants. The *grands seigneurs* wore lynx as a mark of their wealth, and so, over the centuries, did an ever-increasing number of status-hungry bourgeois and *petite noblesse*. Inevitably there was a limit to the amount of luxury the species could support, and by about 1800, the lynx of the Vosges had been wiped out.

In Spain, the cats have done better, but not by much. With a population that currently stands at about one thousand, the Iberian lynx may be the most endangered carnivore in Europe. Despite its ever-decreasing numbers and diminishing habitat, people still break the law to kill it. The only "sense" of the lynx that some people want is its absence.

Happily, the old day is gradually passing, and this brutal attitude, though it still exists, no longer goes unopposed. Across Europe, lynx have been taken off the official hit-lists of animal pests, a change that provides them a measure of belated protection. More significantly, the species has now been restored to a few areas, including the national park of Bavaria. In the most successful of these operations, eighteen cats from Czechoslovakia were transported to Switzerland and, over a period of years, were released in the Jura mountains and Swiss Alps. Since 1971, four of these founding animals (the only four that bred) have given rise to a population of about one hundred.

Although far from restoring what has been lost—nothing can do that now—the reintroductions do signal the growing desire, especially among urban folk, to "rewild" their countryside. In 1987, when three kittens were born to an introduced female lynx in Alsace, the French public beamed like proud godparents. It was, as the local press noted, the first such "happy event" in two hundred years. A few months later, when the mother lynx, Elisa, and an adult male were shot, the papers described their deaths as murders.

If the lynx is in trouble in most of western Europe, its status in eastern Eurasia is virtually unknown. Only in North America are there grounds to think that the cats are in reasonable health. Given that between 5,000 and 50,000 Canadian lynx are "harvested" each year by trappers (many for sale in German markets), the Canadian population likely stands somewhere in the tens or hundreds of thousands, though no one can say with confidence whether the true figure is closer to the bottom or top of this range. For one thing, lynx are almost impossible to count. For another, their numbers fluctuate dramatically, depending on what is happening in their home forest.

North American lynx are specialists. Although they can kill grouse, ducks, mice, beavers, squir-

The lynx of North America, Europe and Asia all look very much the same, with their tufted ears, big feet, long legs and stumpy black-tipped tails. On the basis of these and other similarities, some scientists believe that these cats all belong to one circumpolar species, Felis lynx. *Within this classification, Eurasian, Spanish and North American lynx are recognized as different races, or subspecies, and are known respectively as* Felis lynx lynx, Felis lynx pardina *and* Felis lynx canadensis. *But some experts think these races are sufficiently different from each other that they ought to be recognized as three separate species: the Eurasian, the Spanish and the North American lynx.*

The North American bobcat, with its smaller paws, shorter legs, thinner fur, shorter ear tufts and barred and spotted tail, is different enough from the others that everyone agrees it is a species all on its own. It can be called either Felis rufus *or* Lynx rufus.

rels, even deer, they are critically dependent on a single food—the snowshoe hare. When hares increase in number, North American lynx populations climb. When hare numbers dwindle, the cats follow them into decline. As Ernest Thompson Seton put it, in a typically toothsome phrase, the lynx "lives on Rabbits, follows the Rabbits, thinks Rabbits, tastes like Rabbits, increases with them, and on their failure dies of starvation in the unrabbited woods."

Over the past fifty years, the lynx's changing fortunes have provided ecologists with a major perplexity. The lynx's ups and downs don't occur

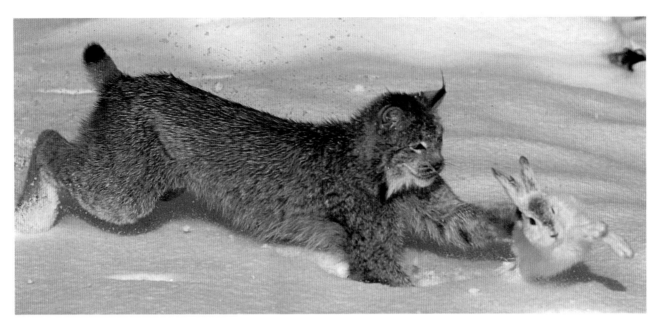

With a final burst of speed, a lynx lunges through the drifts to nab a snowshoe hare. Throughout its range in Europe, Asia and North America, the lynx can be recognized by its black-tipped tail, long legs, tufted ears and "bearded" face. *Tom & Pat Leeson*

at random; instead, they are cyclic. A complete pattern, from peak population down to the trough and back up to the peak, generally takes from eight to eleven years, with an average of about ten. This predictable rhythm can be detected in fur-trade records for more than 250 years and appears to be roughly synchronous over vast areas.

Why would the life of a forest go through such a pulse? Could the cause be epidemics? Trapping? Forest fires? Changes in the sun? Over the years, these explanations and several others have all been examined. Current thinking describes a dynamic interaction amongst the inhabitants of the northern forest. The story begins with willows and other woody plants that produce juicy shoots and bark. Hares eat this nutritious winter browse and have big litters of bunnies, which grow up, eat and have more bunnies, and on and on, until the thickets are literally hopping with long-eared herbivores. Where there are thousands of snowshoe hares, there will be dozens of lynx, enjoying the easy hunting and raising their own large families.

But this widespread abundance depends on the trees and shrubs, which soon somehow determine that they have taken enough. Willows and alders, two of the hare's favourite foods, respond to aggressive browsing by putting out new shoots that contain bitter, indigestible compounds related to turpentine. This change puts the hares into a double bind. Not only has their food supply been reduced in quantity by thousands of gnawing teeth, it has also been diminished in quality by an act of herbal angst. Under these conditions, many hares starve and the survivors reproduce slowly.

By the time the hares reach bottom (at a scant 5 per cent of their top numbers), the lynx have hit hard times, too. The prosperous dozens of the good old days dwindle to a handful of gaunt survivors and footsore wanderers. It's the darkness before dawn. Granted a reprieve from browsing, the shrubs soon begin producing succulent young shoots. Within a couple of years the woods are full of bunnies, and lynx start to raise young kits. The forest's ten-year cycle is on the upsurge again.

Everybody knows, with no-nonsense certainty, that willows, lynx and snowshoe hares are different kinds of creatures and entirely distinct. Willows are bushes. Lynx are cats. Hares are lagomorphs. But this perception of separateness is partly illusory. We can perceive the surfaces that keep things apart, but not the interactions that hold them together. The connections within the forest are real, as substantial as the nerves and arteries that unite our own bodies. Considered all in all and over a period of time, the shrub-hare-lynx interaction is a self-regulating system, a whole within the larger whole of the northern forest.

Because the boreal forest is a simple ecosystem with relatively few species, it is quite easy to describe how the lynx is "wired in" to its circuitry. But the lifelines of the bobcat are more difficult to depict, because the ecosystems in which it lives are typically more complex. The number of species increases the farther south you go, and bobcats range from southern Canada all the way to central Mexico. So unlike northern lynx, with their one-dish menu of hares, bobcats have the advantage of a varied diet: fish, rattlesnakes, meadowlarks, coots, flying squirrels, opossums, woodrats. They also appreciate chickens—a taste that failed to endear them to pioneer settlers—and have long fallen under suspicion of killing "game" animals. Quoth William Wood, whose *New Englands Prospect, a True, Lively, and Experimental Description of that Part of America* was published in 1634:

The wilde cat useth to kill Deare, which hee thus effecteth: Knowing the Deares tracts, hee will lye lurking in long weedes, the Deare passing by he suddenly leapes upon his backe, from thence gets to his necke, and scratcheth out his throate; he hath likewise a devise to get Geese, for being much of the colour of a Goose he will place himselfe close by the water, holding up his bob taile, which is like a Goose necke; the Geese seeing this counterfet Goose, approach nigh to visit him, who with a suddain jerke apprehends his mistrustlesse prey.

For such "crimes," real and imagined, bobcats were held under bounty for about three hundred years and are still listed as vermin in parts of Texas.

Although Wood's tall-tail tale is itself a "counterfet," his deer-hunt story has a basis in fact. A bobcat, an animal about twice the size of a domestic cat, actually can take down mature ungulates. It is as if Puss gave up on birds and started dragging home freshly killed golden retrievers. Not surprisingly, a deer-hunting bobcat is often in for a very rough experience. By studying tracks in the snow, cat researcher Gary Koehler reconstructed one episode in the Salmon River Mountains of Idaho, in which a female bobcat—probable weight 8 kilograms (about 20 pounds)—leaped on the back of a deer and hung on, ride-'em-cowboy style, as "the deer bounded down the rugged slope, dodging around bluffs, bolting through bushes and up against trees. The ride ended some 300 feet below at the foot of the slope, where perhaps the deer stumbled, giving the cat time to grasp the deer's throat in its mouth for a suffocating bite." Needless to say, deer are not the bobcat's preferred prey, though they can form a critical part of its wintertime fare in some regions.

Overall, however, the prey that suits the bobcat best is the local lagomorph, be it a jackrabbit, a snowshoe hare or, most often, a cottontail. These animals are small enough to be killed easily and

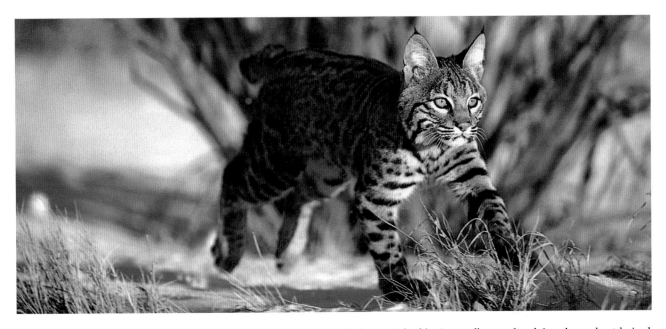

Similar in size and shape to the North American lynx, the bobcat is distinguished by its small ear tufts, dainty legs, short-haired coat and elegant markings. Although able to cope with light snow, the bobcat prefers the fair weather zones of southern Canada and the United States. *Denver Bryan*

large enough to provide a bobcat with a day or two's sustenance. Where rabbits and hares are plentiful, bobcats reproduce quickly. When rabbits and hares are scarce, the cats usually produce very few offspring. (Because bobcats can turn to other prey during low-rabbit years, their ups and downs are usually more subtle than those suffered by lynx.) As one might expect, bobcats generally favour shrublands and open forests where one or another of their preferred food animals is abundant—coulees, streambeds, patches of brush; hedgerows, pastures, swamps and marshes; roadsides, abandoned fields and regenerating clearcuts.

Although bobcats have been eliminated from some east-coast states by urban sprawl and from the mid-west by the "let-nothing-go-unplowed" mode of agriculture, they still occupy most of their original range. In fact, they have probably increased in both numbers and area overall, as logging and small-scale farming have created open woodlands. At the northern edge of their distribution, they even seem to be edging into what was once exclusive lynx range. Do the lynx leave first, alienated by human disturbance? Or do the bobcats invade and actively push the lynx back?

Although bobcats are about the same size as lynx, they are much scrappier. "I have no idea what a bobcat-lynx encounter looks like," admits Canadian Wildlife Service biologist Gerry Parker, "but it may be a matter of the two meeting one-on-one, the bobcat asserting its dominance [through body language and snarls], and the lynx slinking off to occupy some other territory." Parker surmises that this bloodless conflict may be the means by which bobcats have recently displaced lynx from most of Cape Breton, a 4,000-square-kilometre (1,500-square-mile) island in the Gulf of St. Lawrence. Lynx were the only wild cats on Cape Breton until 1955, when a causeway was built to the mainland and the bobcats padded across. Today bobcats have taken over three-quarters of the island and lynx have become uncommon, except in the spruce forests of the Cape Breton highlands. There, at least, lynx have the advantage, with cold-proof furs and snowshoe feet that help them meet the challenges of the north country.

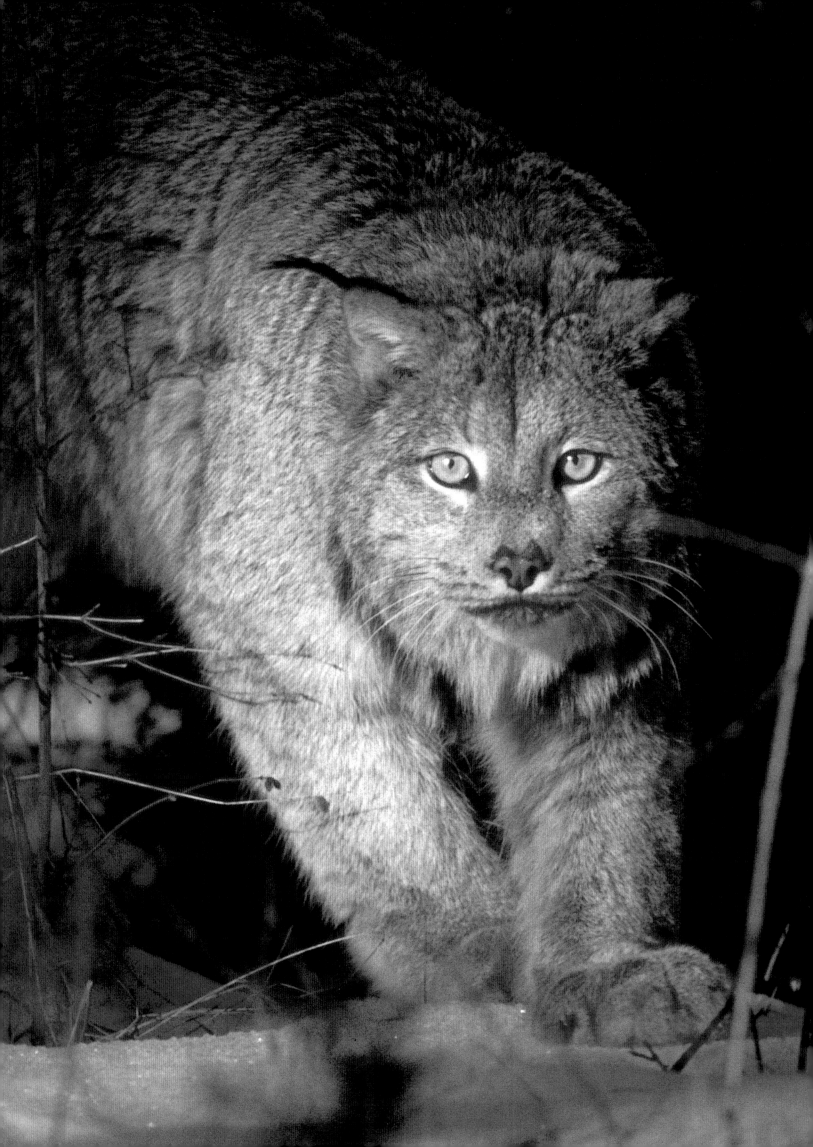

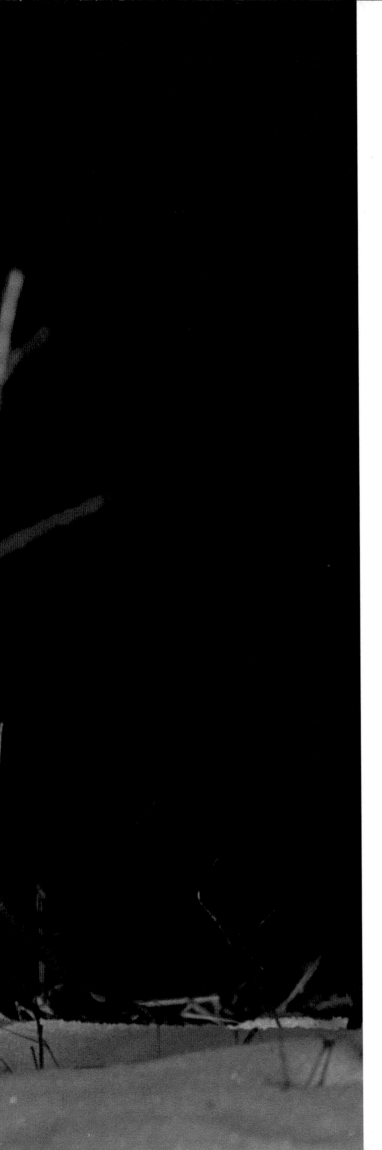

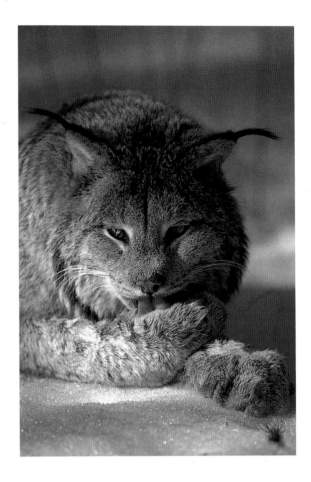

With their dense fur, long legs and snowshoe paws, lynx are perfectly adapted for life in the deep north. Above, a lynx rests peacefully on a bed of snow. Left, a lynx slides into a sudden shaft of light as it pads across the drifts of its home forest. Above and left: Tom Walker

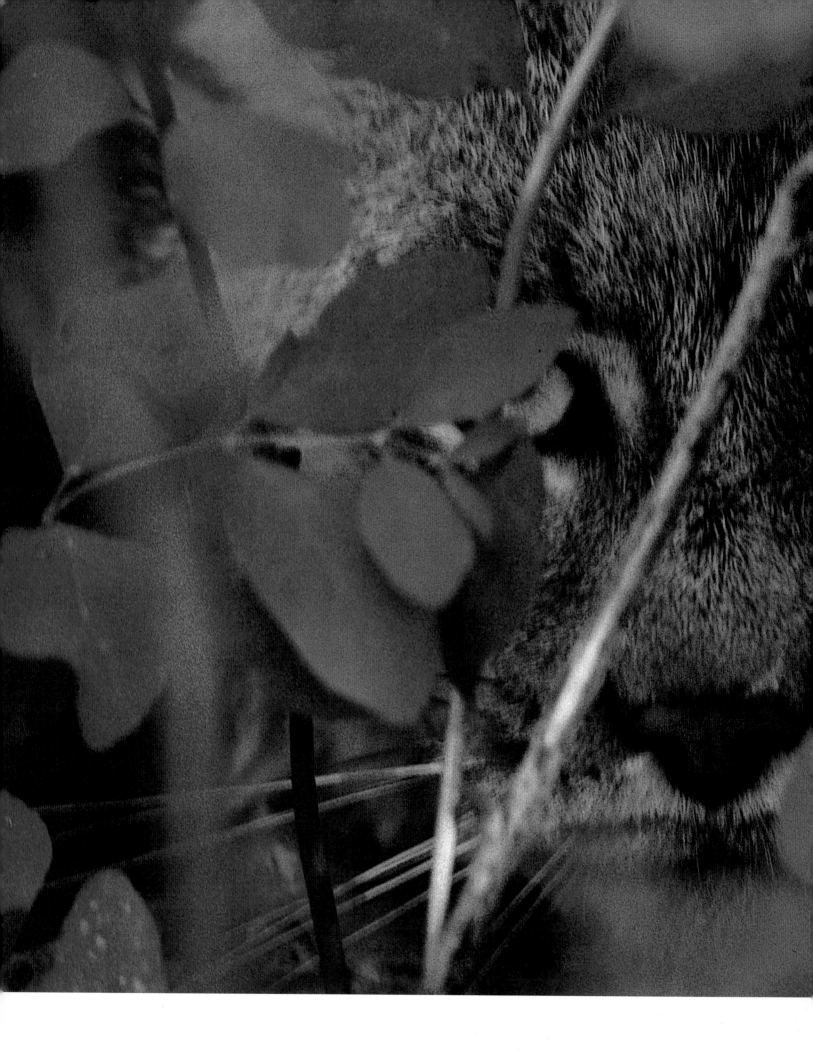

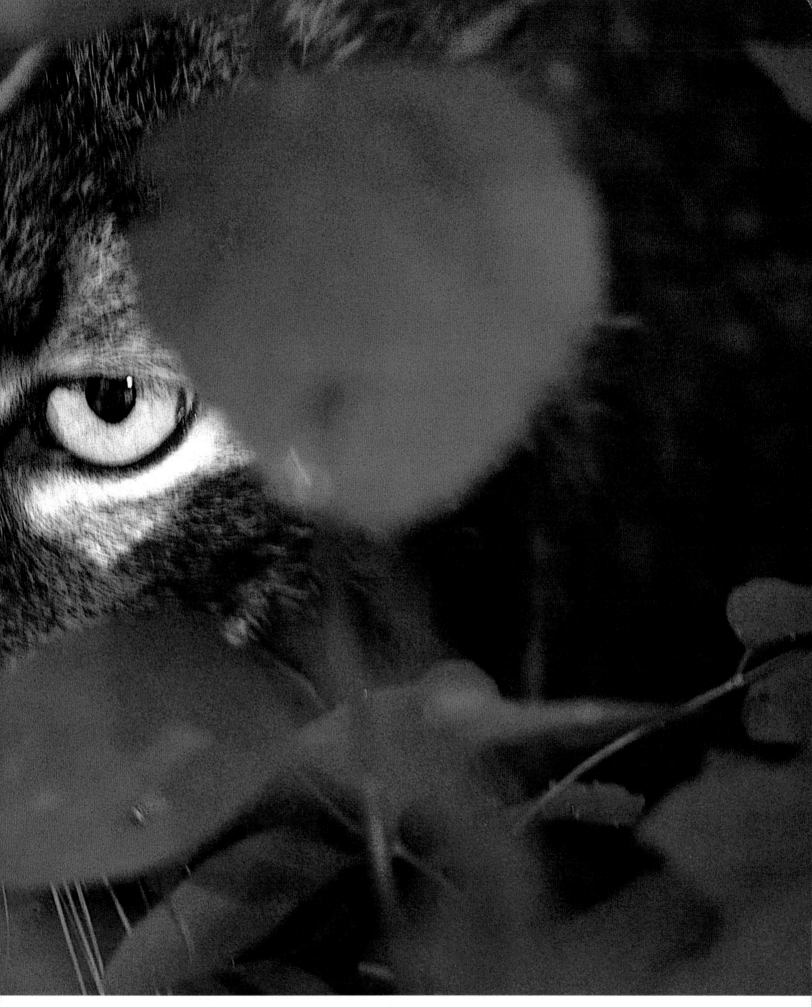

Owl-eyed, a lynx peers through a screen of leaves. Although lynx have good vision in daylight, they are especially gifted at seeing through near-darkness. Their eyes need only one-sixth as much light as our own. Accordingly, they are most active at dawn and dusk and pass their days resting in sheltered thickets. Erwin & Peggy Bauer

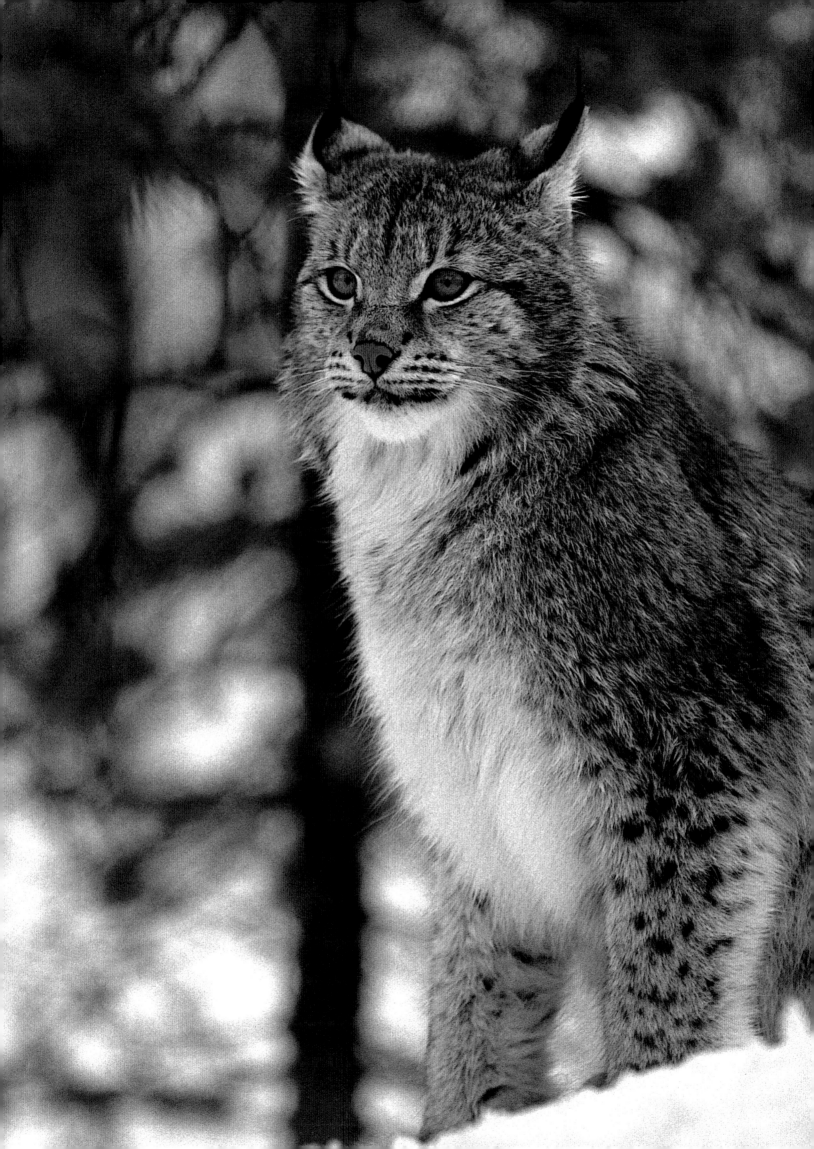

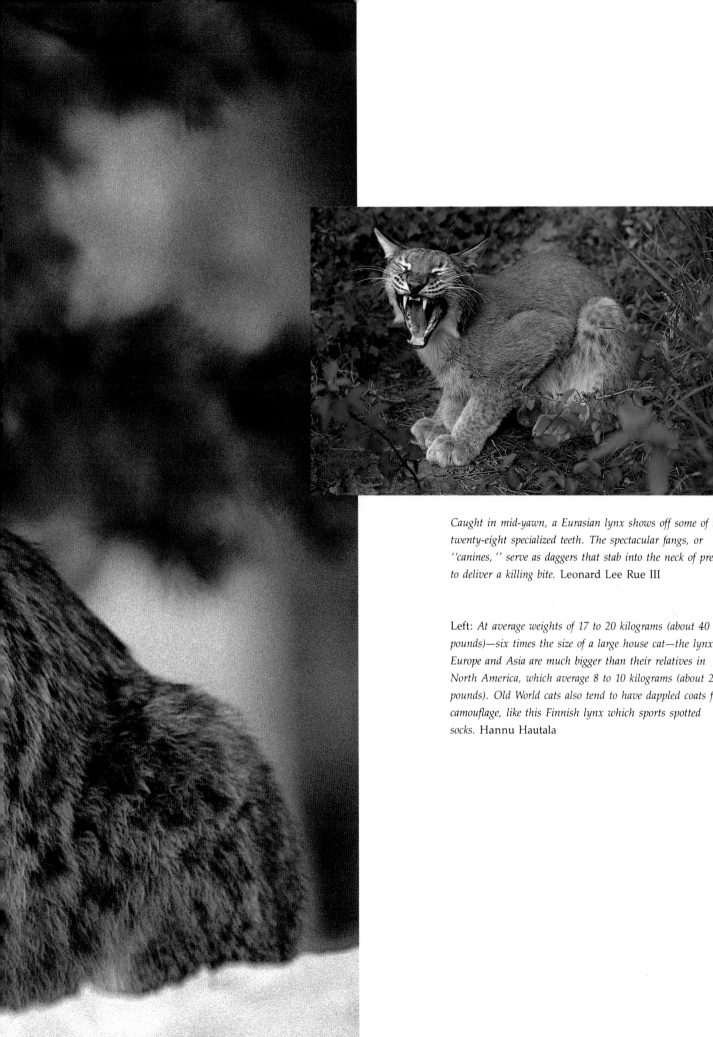

Caught in mid-yawn, a Eurasian lynx shows off some of its twenty-eight specialized teeth. The spectacular fangs, or ''canines,'' serve as daggers that stab into the neck of prey to deliver a killing bite. Leonard Lee Rue III

Left: *At average weights of 17 to 20 kilograms (about 40 pounds)—six times the size of a large house cat—the lynx of Europe and Asia are much bigger than their relatives in North America, which average 8 to 10 kilograms (about 20 pounds). Old World cats also tend to have dappled coats for camouflage, like this Finnish lynx which sports spotted socks.* Hannu Hautala

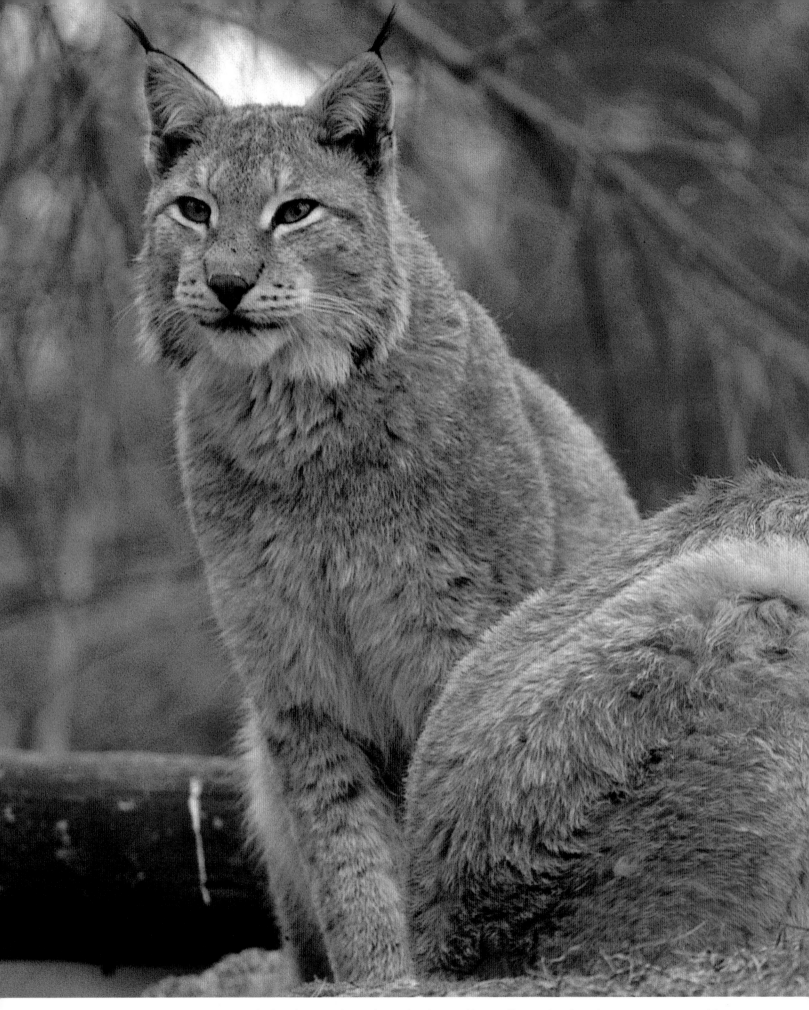

Once plentiful throughout Europe, the lynx is now endangered or extinct in most "western" countries. Over the past twenty years, with much human help, small breeding populations have been re-established in parts of Switzerland, France, Italy, Germany and Slovenia (the northwest corner of former Yugoslavia). John Cancalosi/Valan Photos

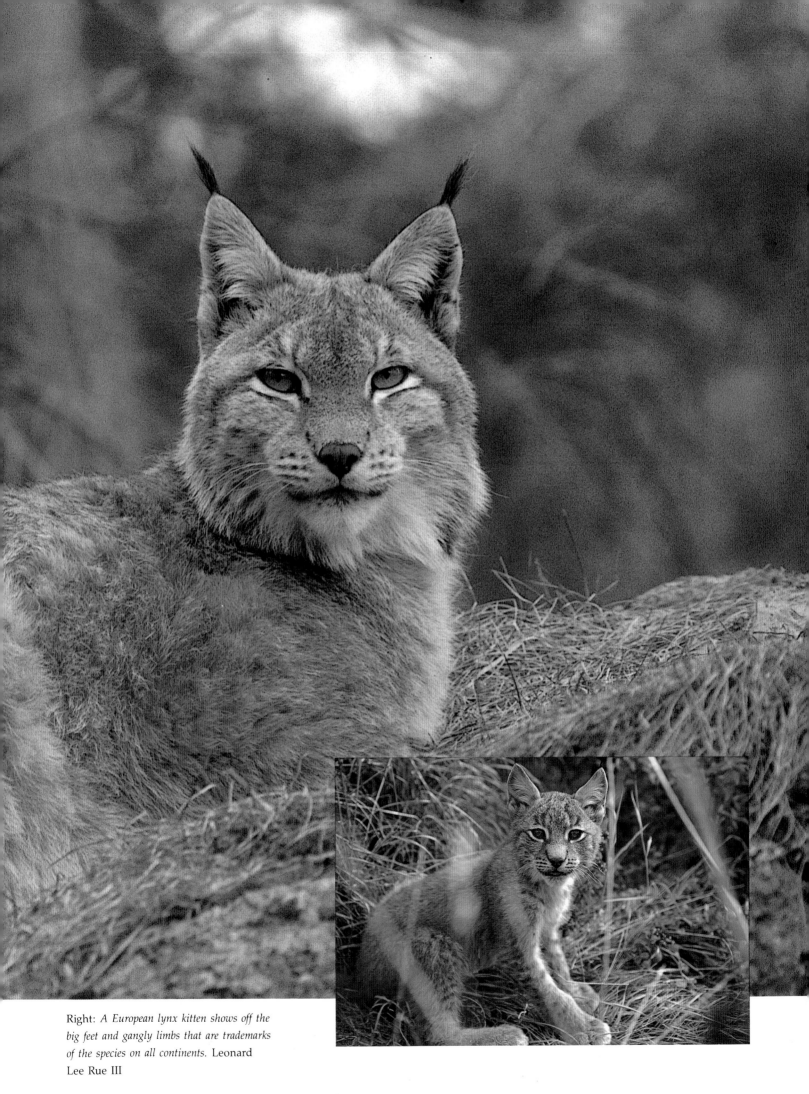

Right: *A European lynx kitten shows off the big feet and gangly limbs that are trademarks of the species on all continents.* Leonard Lee Rue III

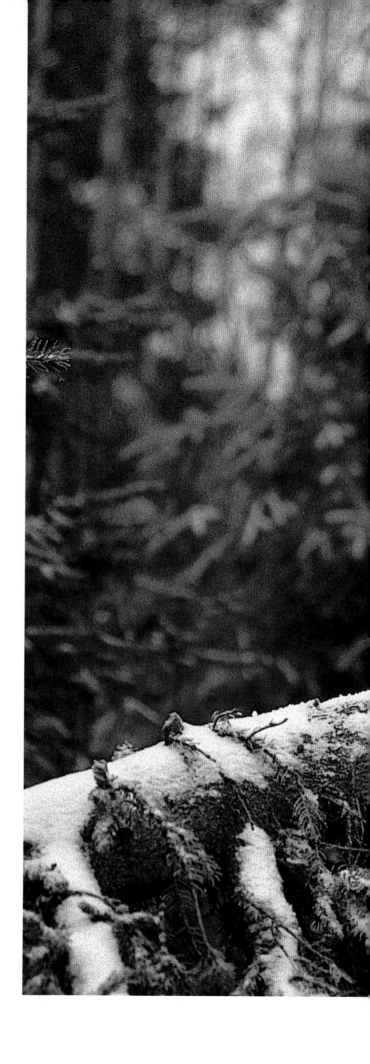

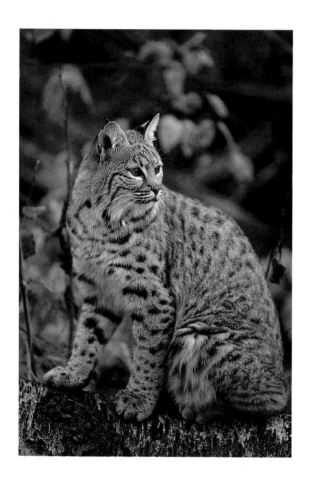

In Eurasia, lynx range south to Spain and Iran, but in North America, they are restricted to the northern forests. Southerly latitudes are occupied by the closely related bob-cat, shown above. Scientists think bobcats descended from Eurasian lynx that crossed the Bering land-bridge during a break in the Ice Ages. North American lynx probably made the trip much later, after bobcats had laid claim to southerly regions. Wayne Lynch

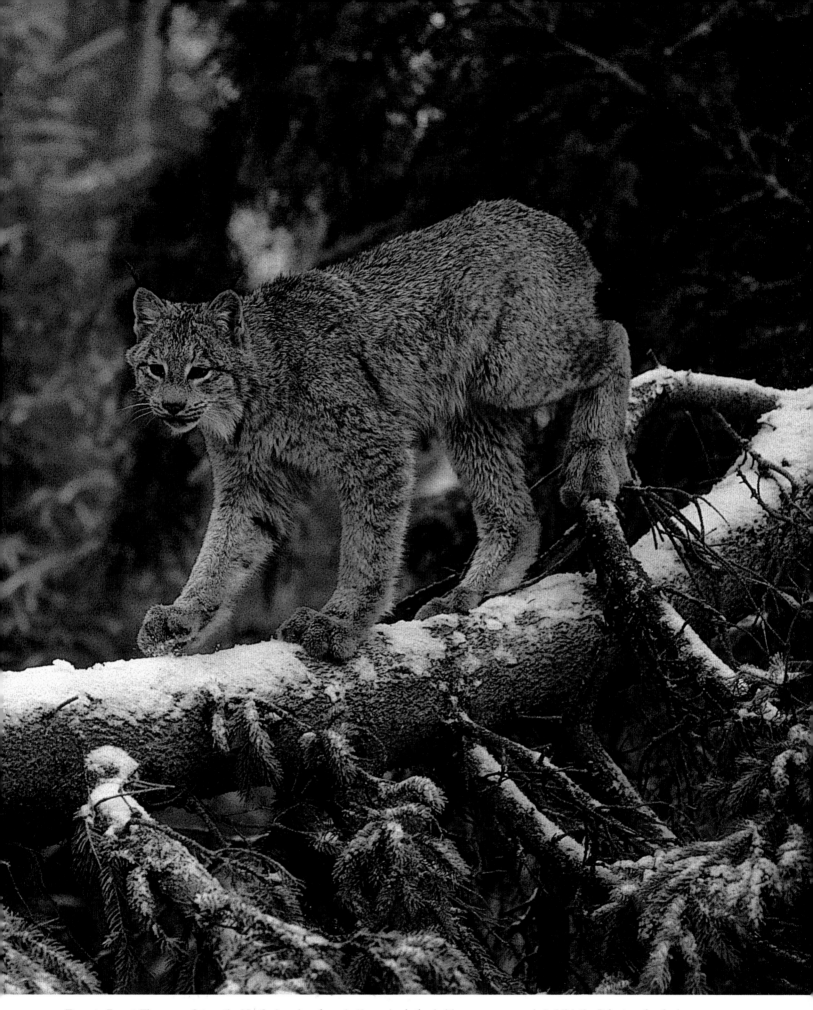

To quote Ernest Thompson Seton, the North American lynx is ''an animal of primitive evergreen woods [while] the Bobcat prefers broken woods....Otherwise expressed, the Lynx is a Cat of the big timber and a Canadian climate; the Bobcat is a Cat of the little timber and a United States climate.'' Here a lynx makes its way through Seton's big timber. Erwin & Peggy Bauer

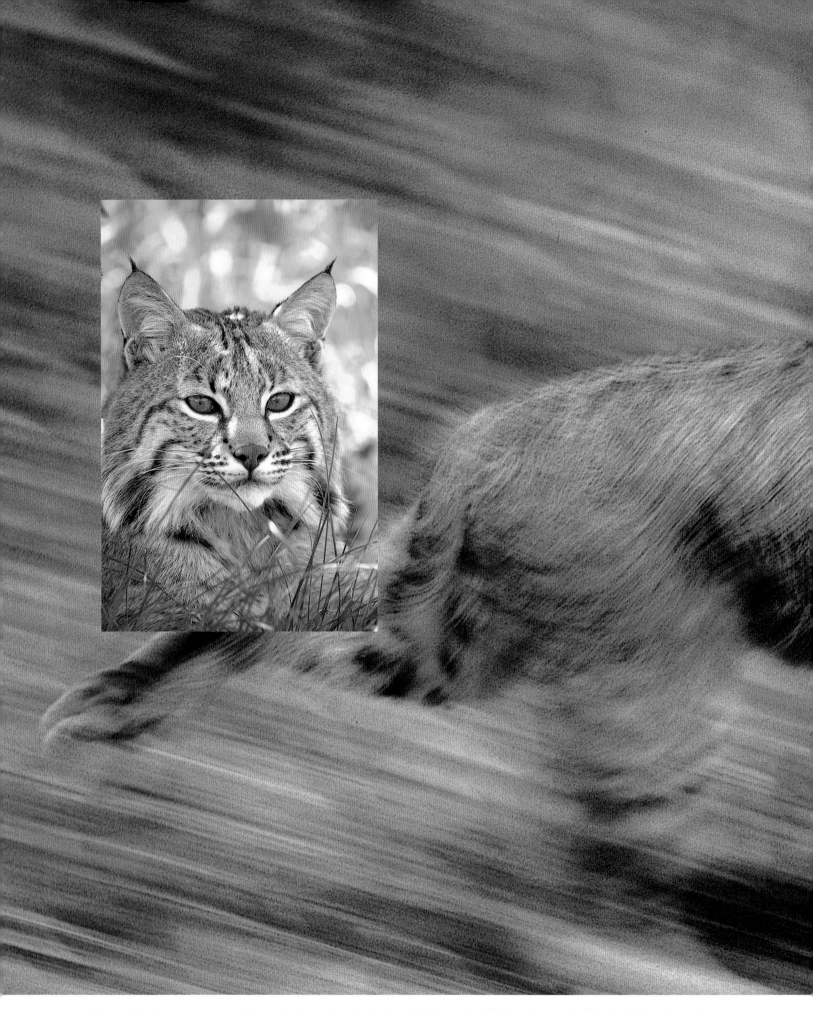

Inset: *Attentive even at rest, a bobcat cocks its ear to catch the tiny, telltale sounds of birds, rodents and rabbits, including ultrasonic (high-pitched) squeaks that are beyond the range of our own hearing.* Stephen J. Krasemann/Valan Photos

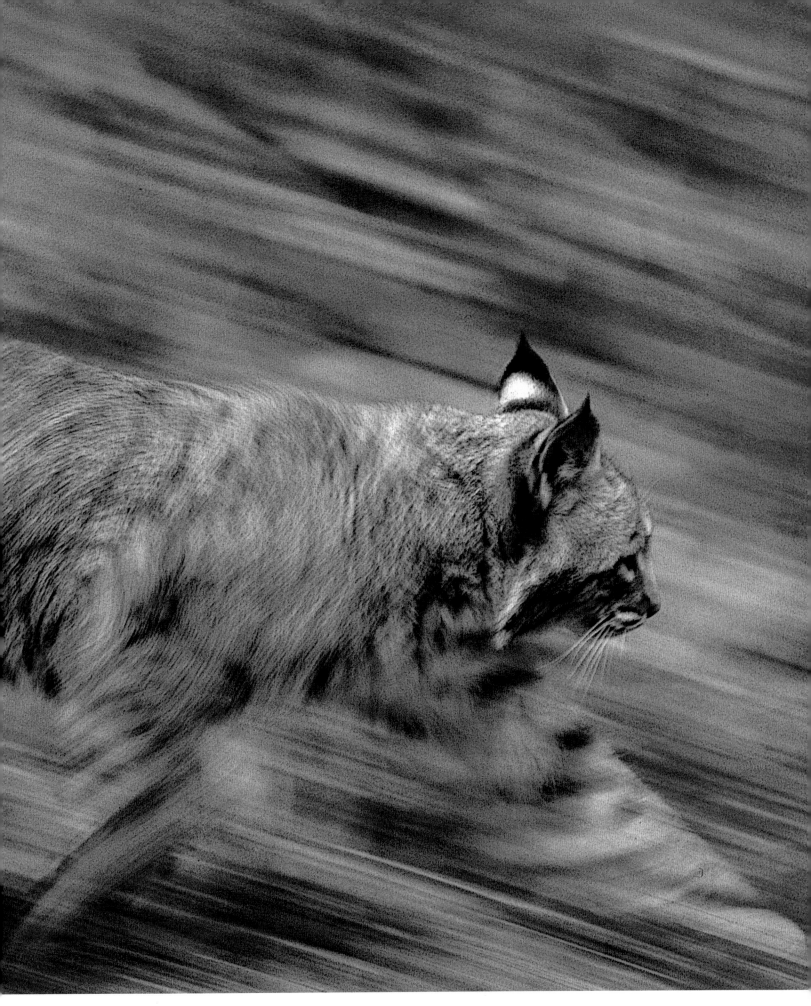

With supple, athletic bodies that have been perfected over 12 million years, cats have been described as the world's most perfect predators. The black-and-white pattern on the bobcat's ears probably helps young cats to keep track of their mothers in the rush of the hunt. Tom & Pat Leeson

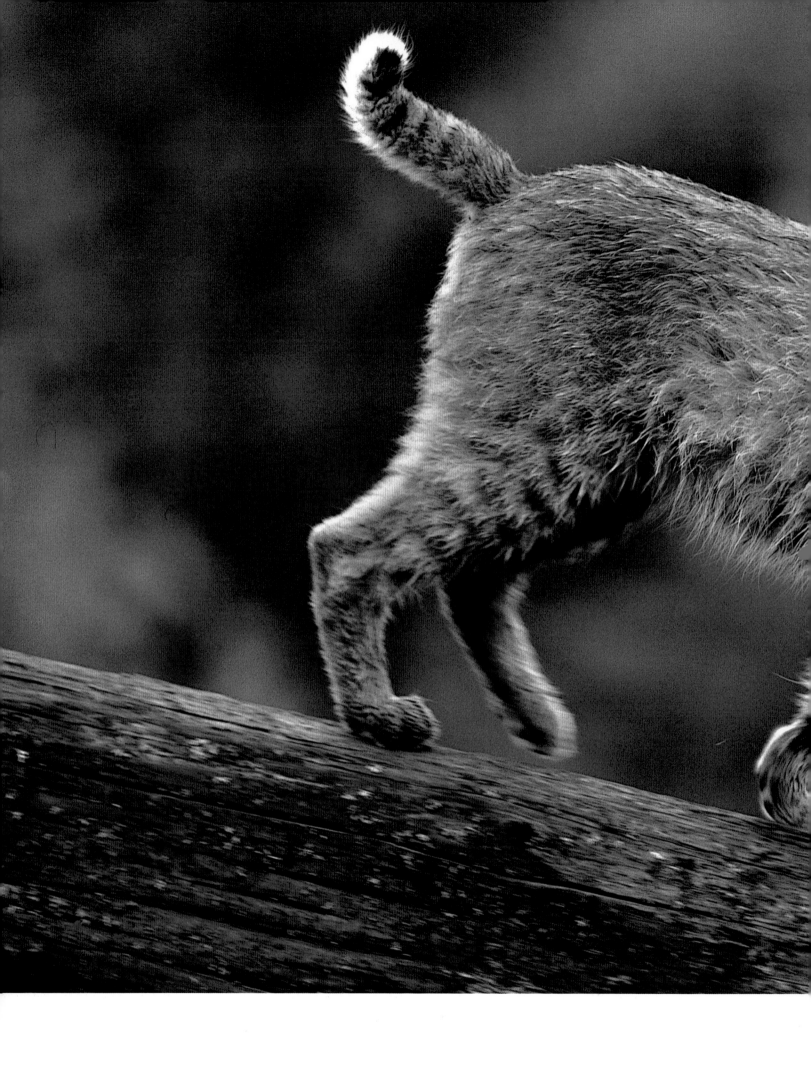

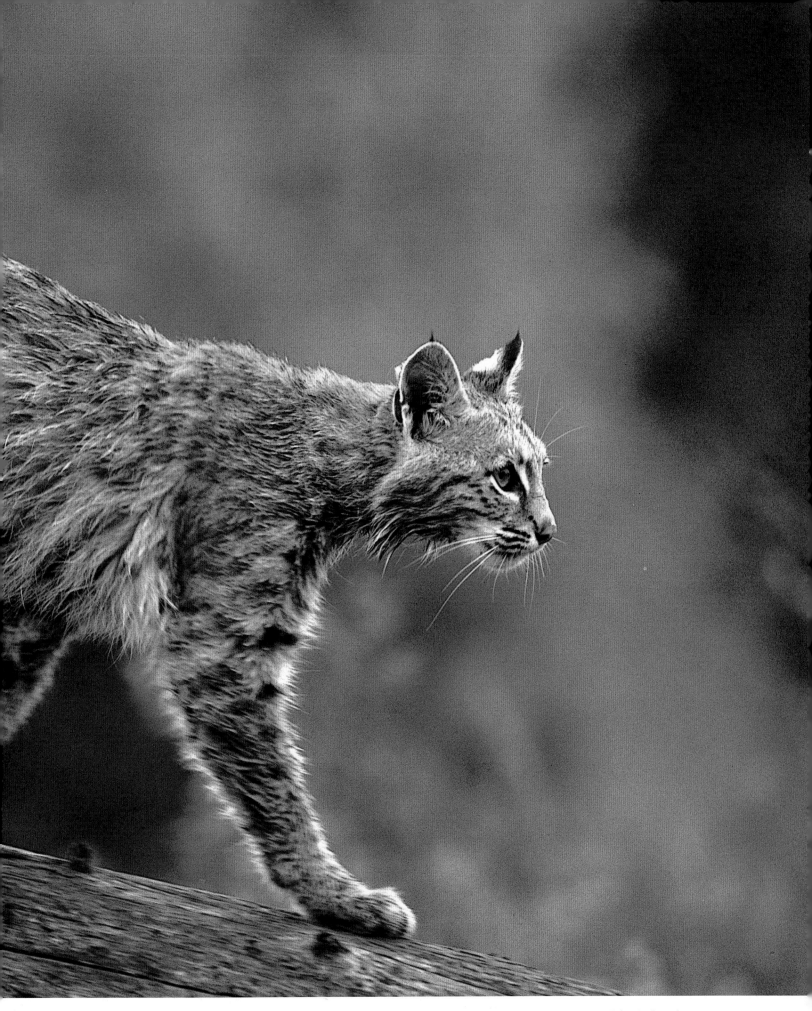

In the summer, the bobcat's soft, luminous fur takes on a reddish tinge, a trait that is acknowledged in the Latin name Felis *(or* Lynx*)* rufus—*the red lynx. (The winter coat tends to be more greyish.) The markings on the tail—barred on top and white beneath—are another important bobcat characteristic. On lynx, the tail is completely black at the tip.* Joe McDonald

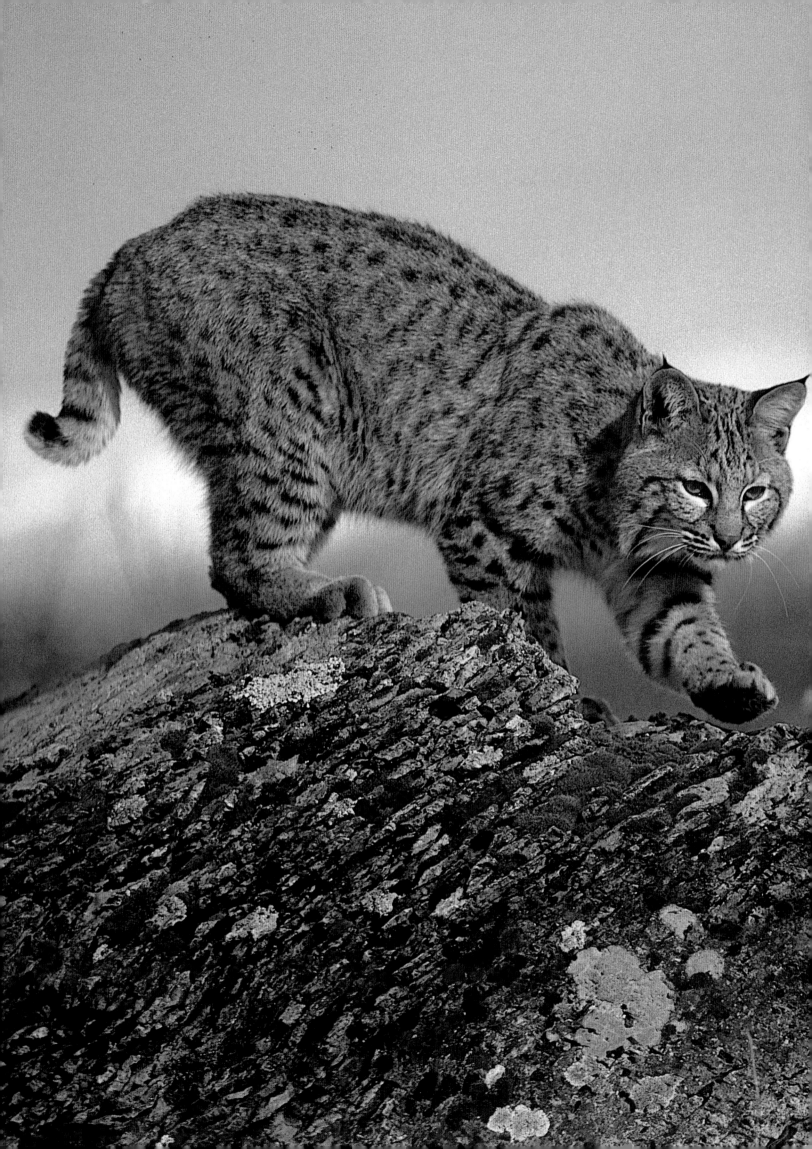

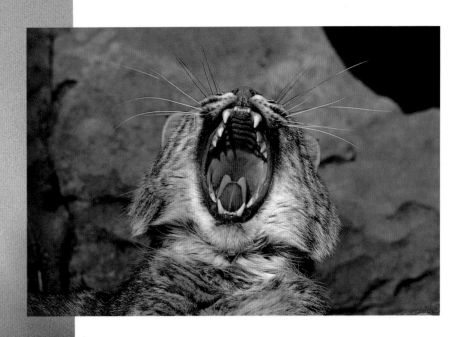

With a mighty yawn, a bobcat reveals some of the "gadgetry" that equips cats to be predators. The rasplike ridges on the roof of the mouth grind up bone and hide. The whiskers are a sensory organ—with a brain-link to the eyes—that help the cat to aim its mouth for a quick-killing bite. Leonard Lee Rue III

Left: Bobcats often favour rocky, broken countryside that offers crevices and rock piles for denning and shelter, plus protective cover for stalking prey. Kent & Donna Dannen

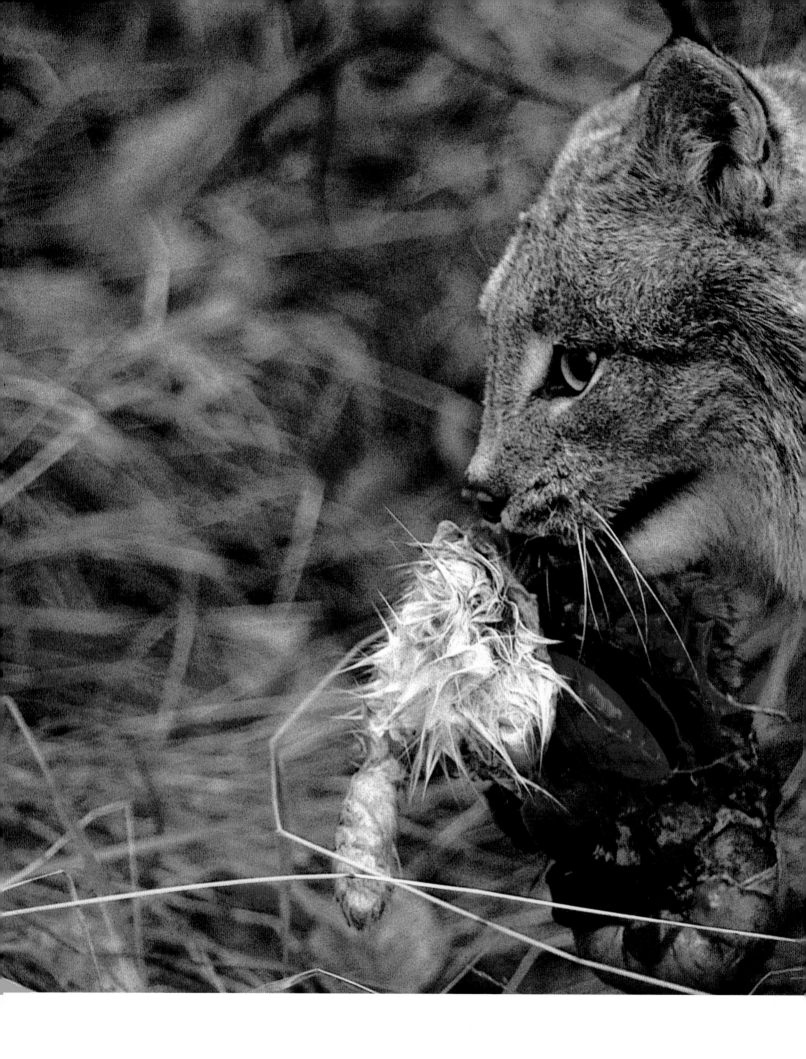

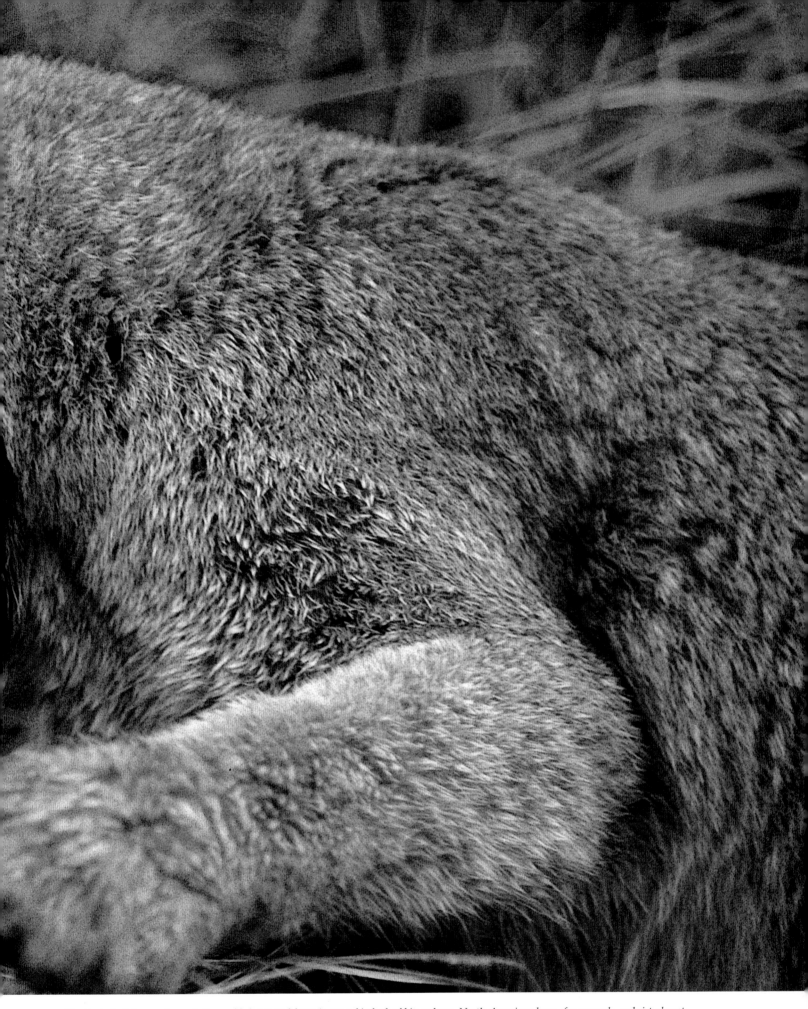

The basic food for most populations of bobcats and lynx is some kind of rabbit or hare. North American lynx, for example, subsist almost exclusively on snowshoe hares, though they also eat mice, voles, squirrels, grouse, ptarmigan and, rarely, caribou, moose or deer. Eurasian lynx, being larger, regularly take deer, but they still rely on rabbits and hares as their staple food. Erwin & Peggy Bauer

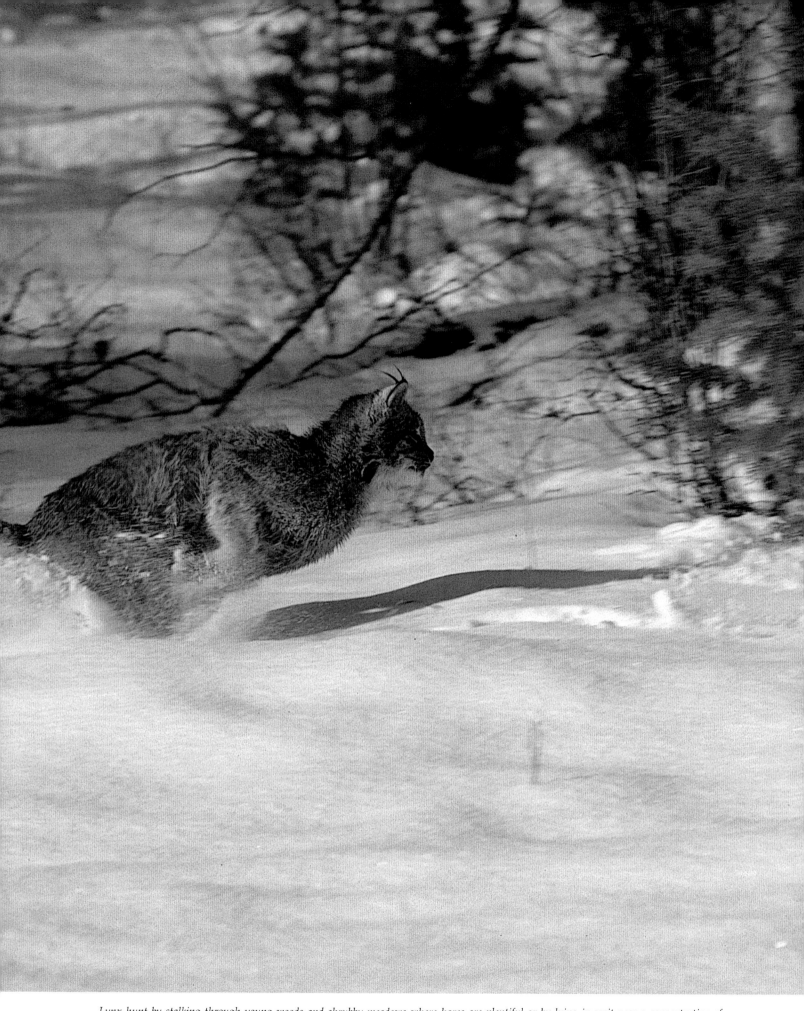

Lynx hunt by stalking through young woods and shrubby meadows where hares are plentiful or by lying in wait near a concentration of hare trails. At the last minute, they close on their prey with sudden power. Tom & Pat Leeson

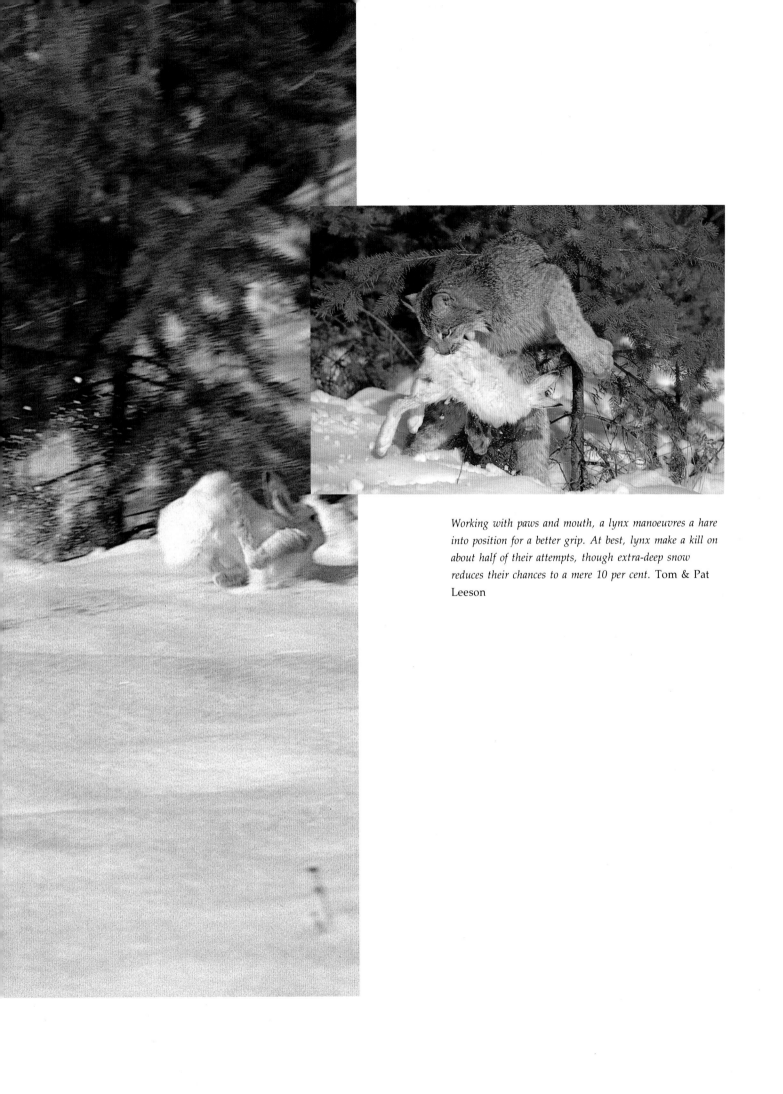

Working with paws and mouth, a lynx manoeuvres a hare into position for a better grip. At best, lynx make a kill on about half of their attempts, though extra-deep snow reduces their chances to a mere 10 per cent. Tom & Pat Leeson

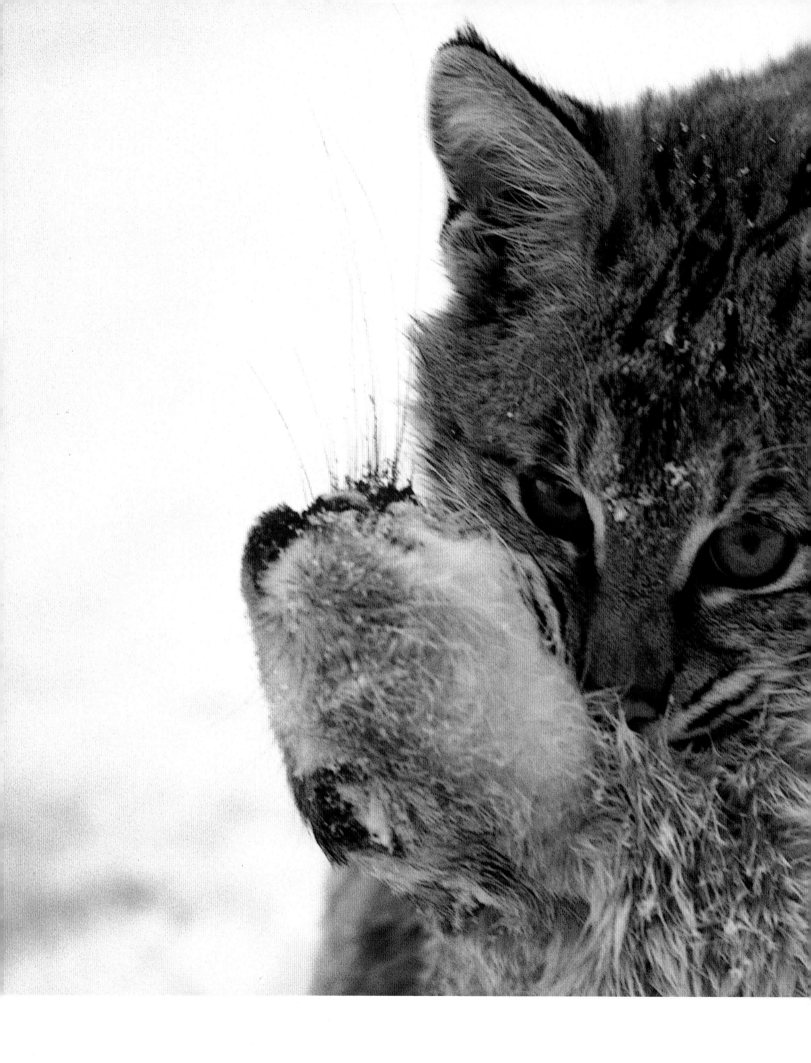

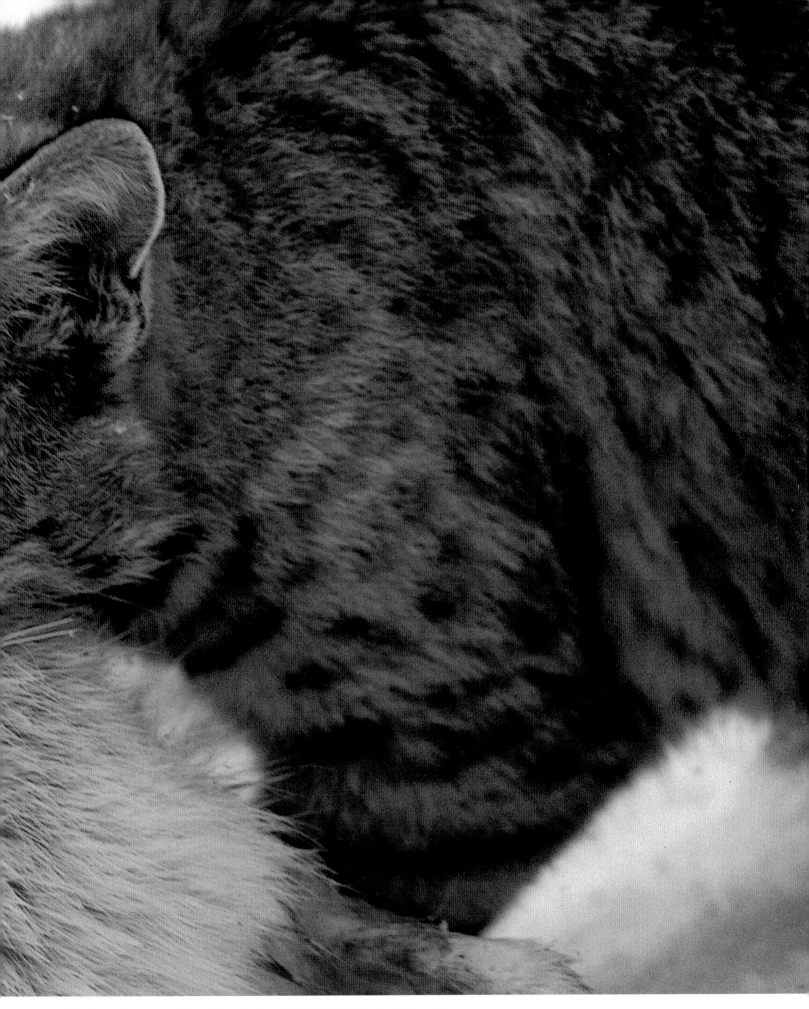

The picture of success: a bobcat clasps the throat of a jackrabbit. Erwin & Peggy Bauer

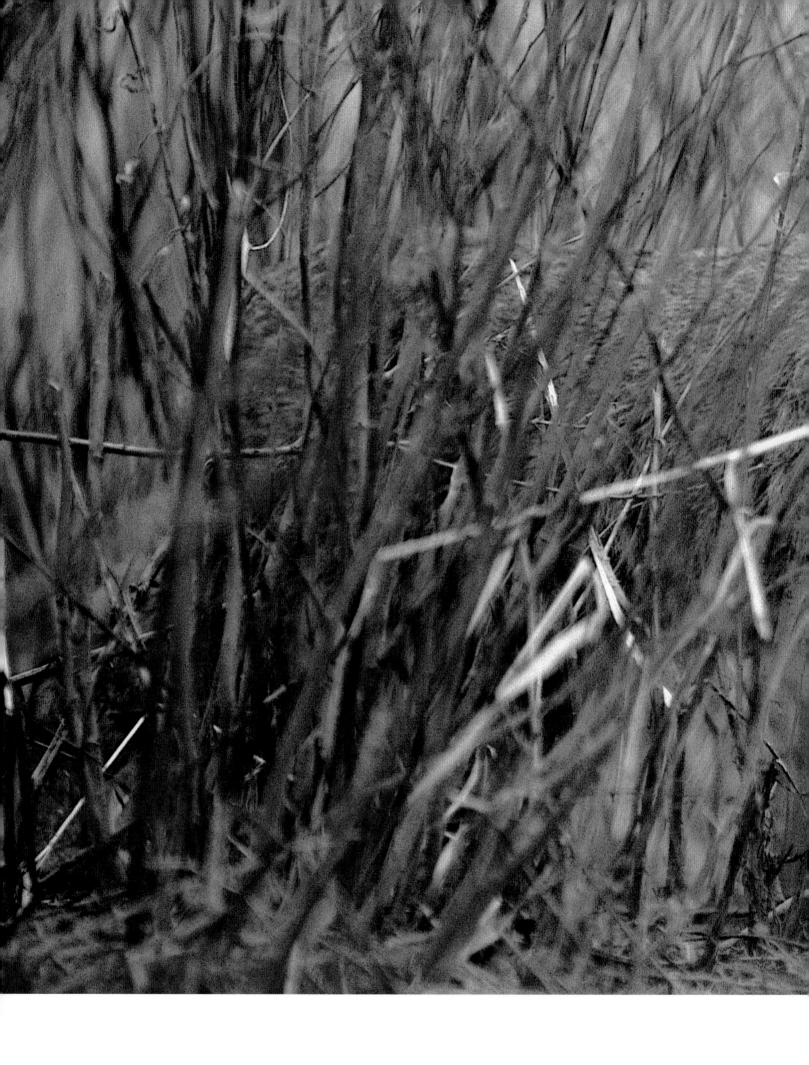

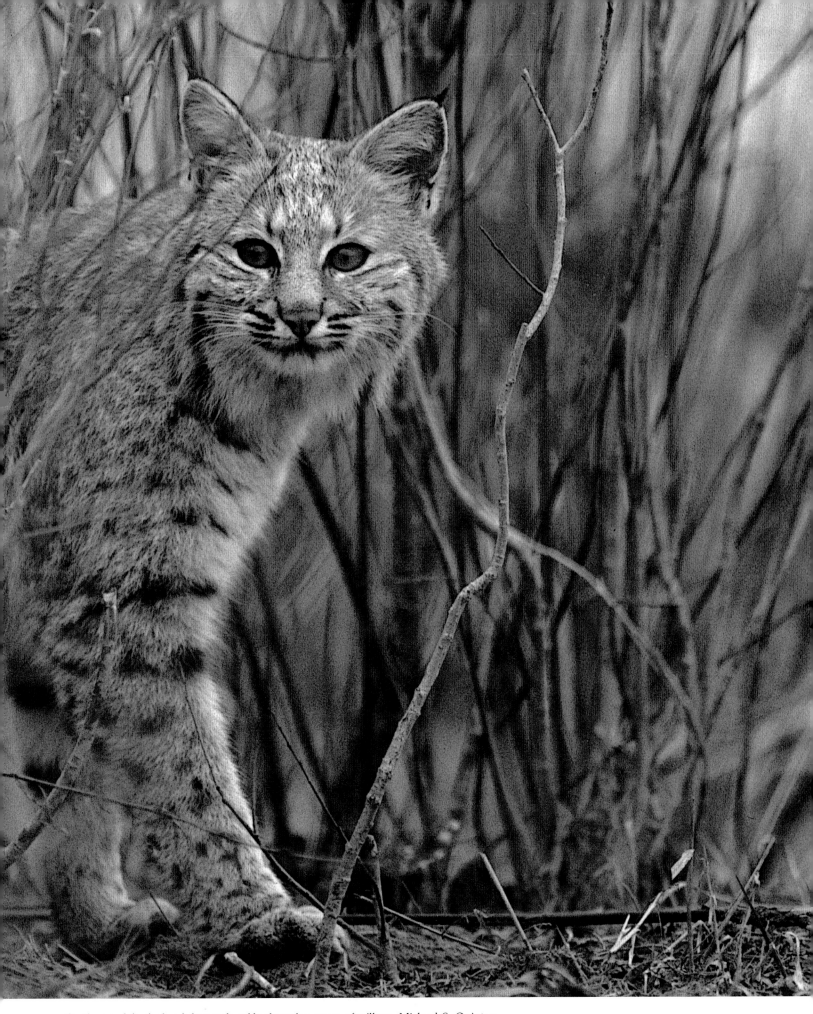

On the prowl for food, a bobcat pads softly through a screen of willows. Michael S. Quinton

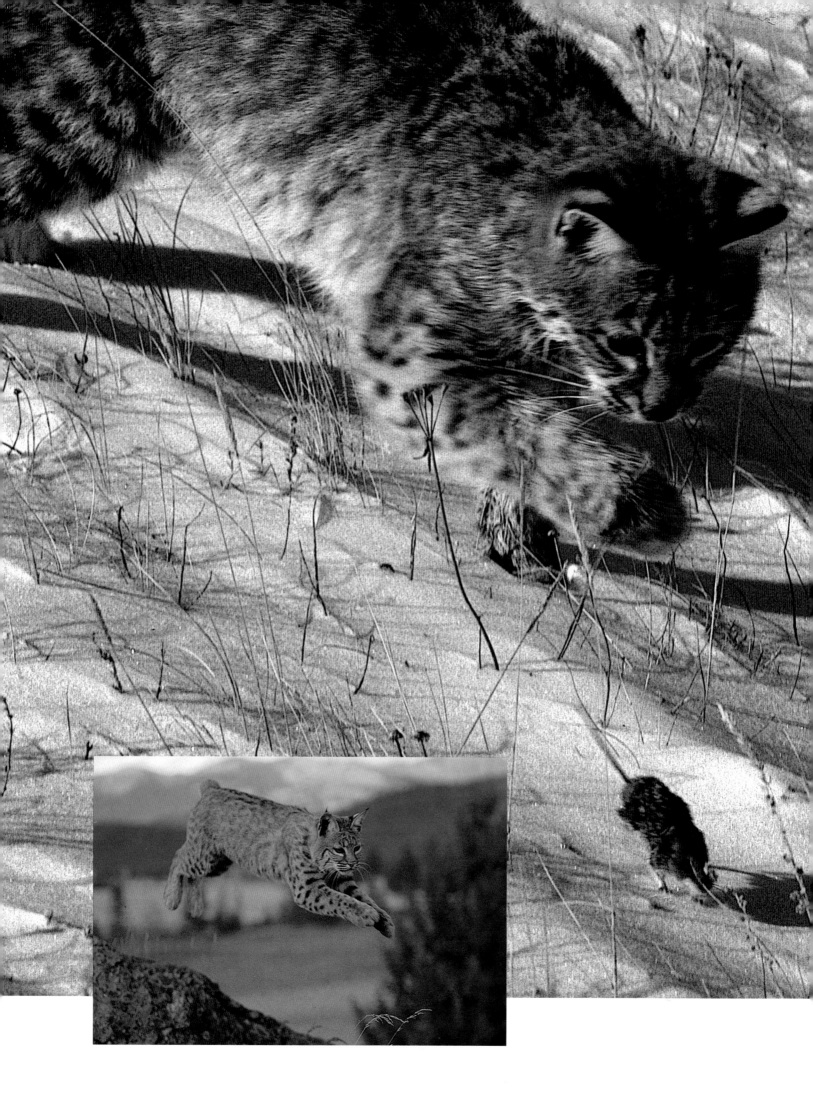

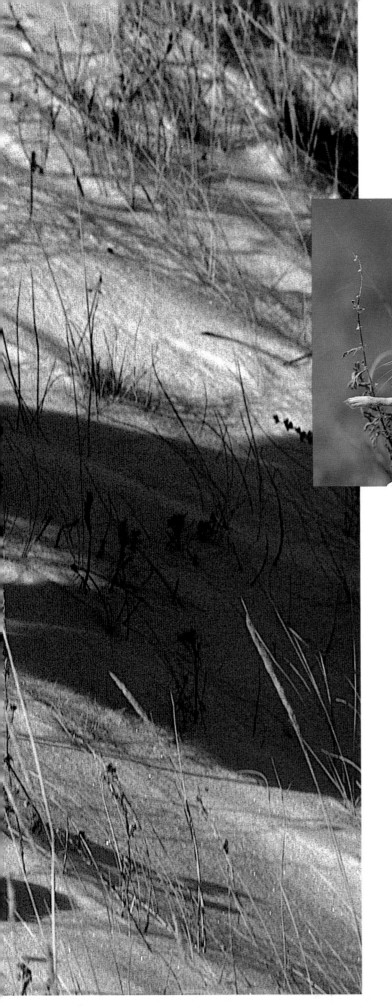

On the sagebrush flats of Colorado, U.S.A., a bobcat prepares to snack on a kangaroo rat. It would take two dozen small rodents—or one rabbit—to provide a day's sustenance. W. Perry Conway

Left: The old cat-and-mouse game. In regions where bobcats subsist on small rodents, each cat requires a hunting ground of some 200 square kilometres (80 square miles). But where rabbit-sized prey is plentiful, a bobcat can often meet its needs within the reach of a city block. Erwin & Peggy Bauer

Inset: A bobcat slinks to within striking distance of its prey or lies in ambush until its quarry comes close. Then, with a twitch of its stubby tail, the cat explodes into action. Alan & Sandy Carey

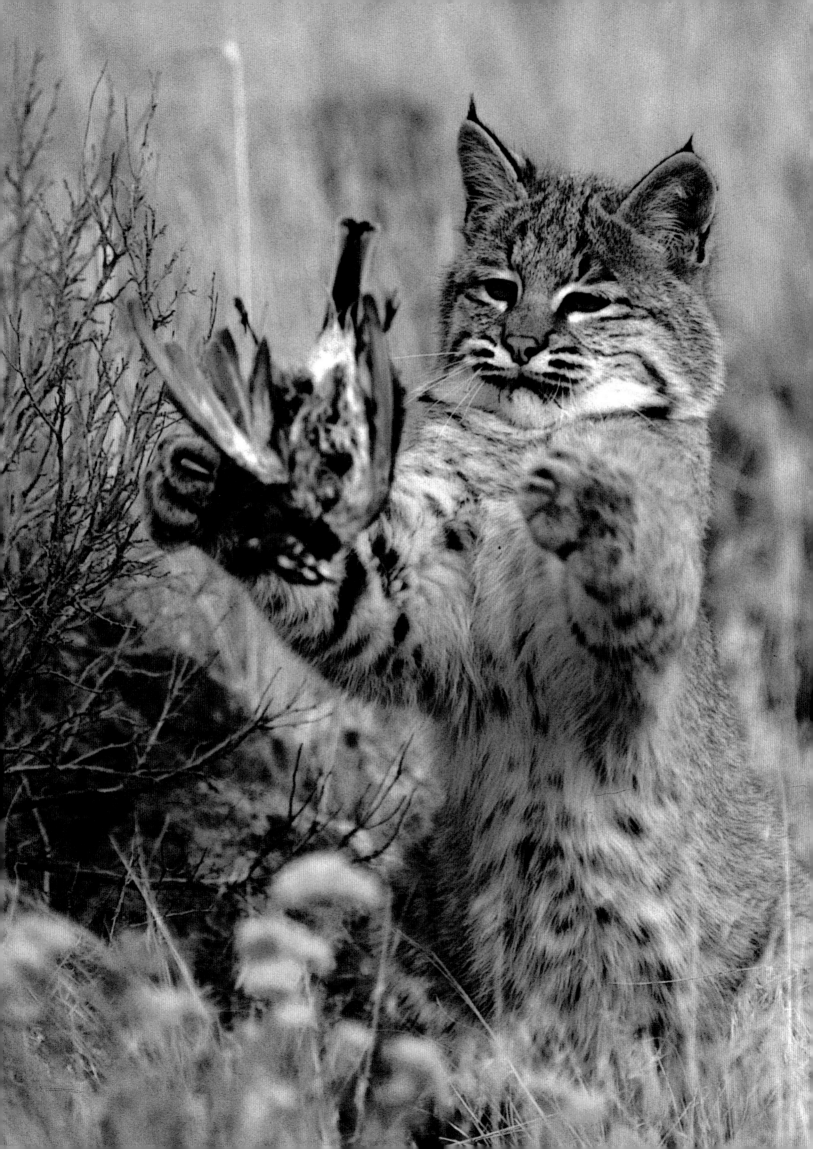

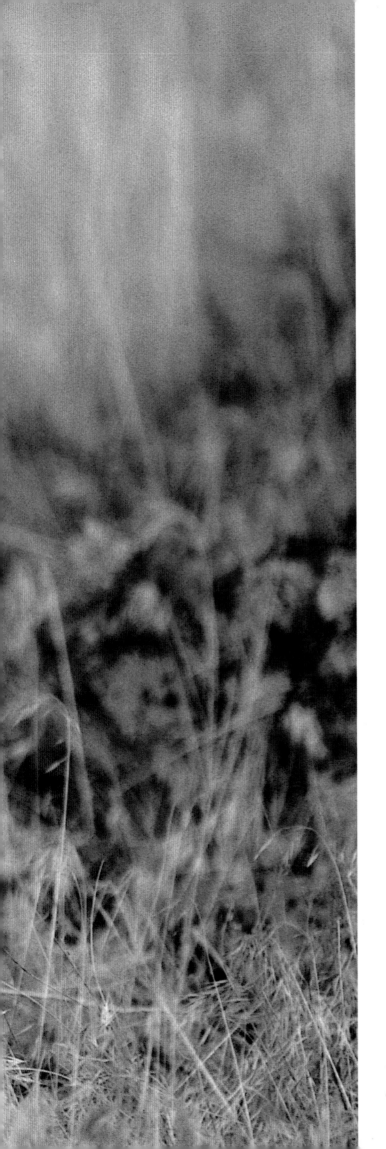

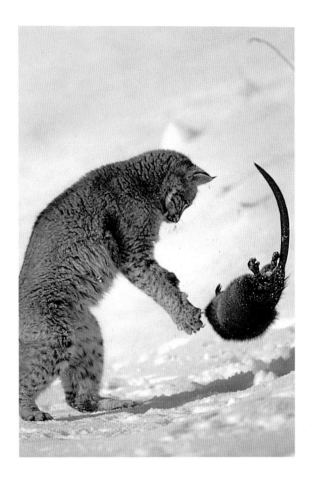

As if to extend the pleasure of hunting, wild cats play with their prey. Here, a bobcat puts a spin on a dead muskrat. Many populations of bobcats enjoy a varied diet that features cotton rats in the southeastern United States and woodrats in the southwest. Muskrats are one of many occasional food items in the bobcat's diet. Michael S. Quinton

Left: A bobcat concentrates its attention on a pre-lunch game of catch with a dead horned lark. Unlike domestic cats, wild felines rarely play with live prey. Michael S. Quinton

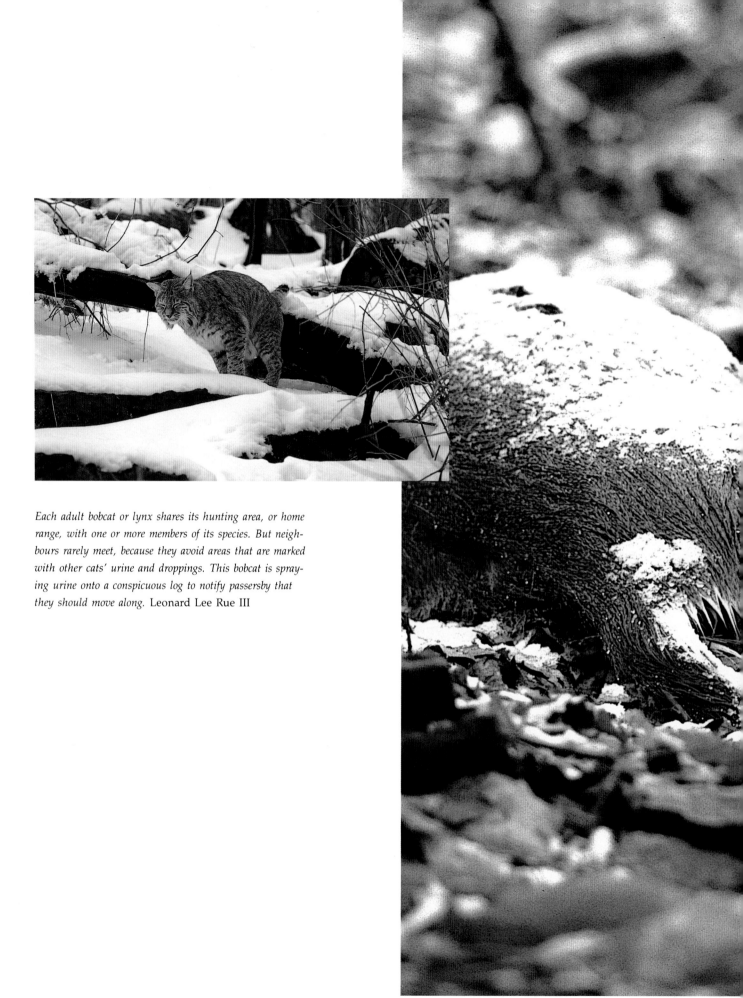

Each adult bobcat or lynx shares its hunting area, or home range, with one or more members of its species. But neighbours rarely meet, because they avoid areas that are marked with other cats' urine and droppings. This bobcat is spraying urine onto a conspicuous log to notify passersby that they should move along. Leonard Lee Rue III

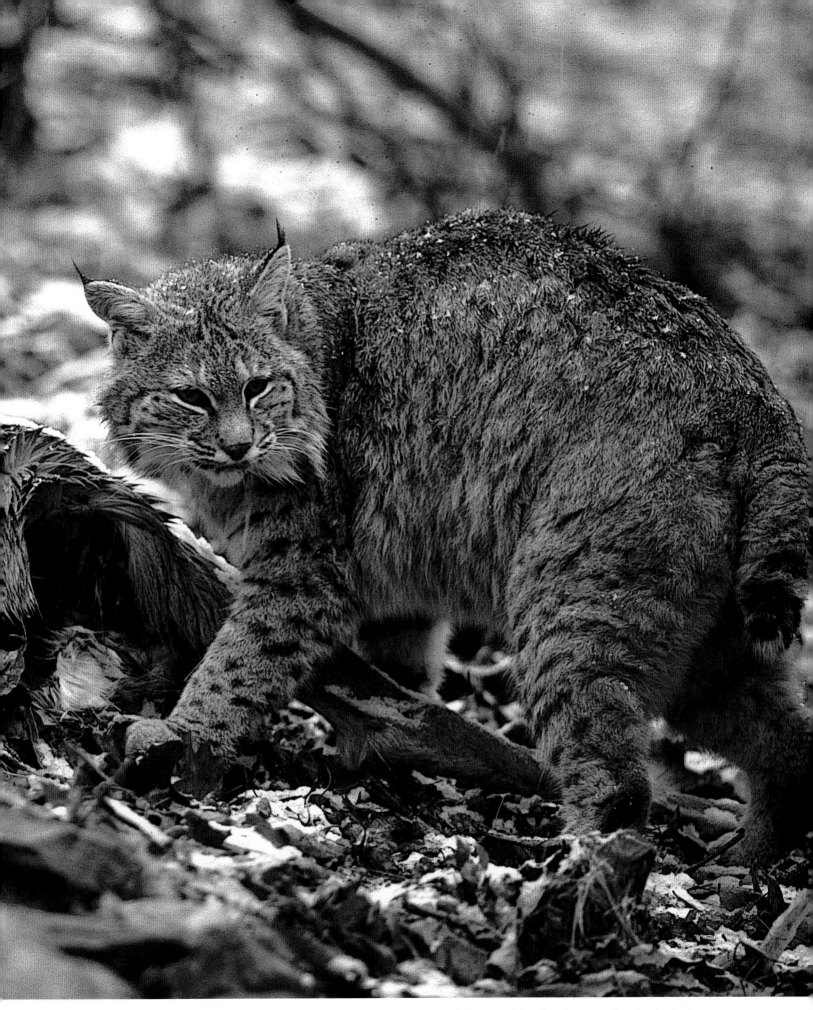

Despite a five-fold difference in weight, bobcats have been known to wrestle down adult deer, especially when deep snow impedes the deer's escape. But even under the most favourable conditions, the little cats are likely to take young, sick or malnourished deer or to acquire the meat as carrion (often animals left behind by "sportsmen"). Mark Wilson/Leonard Rue Enterprises

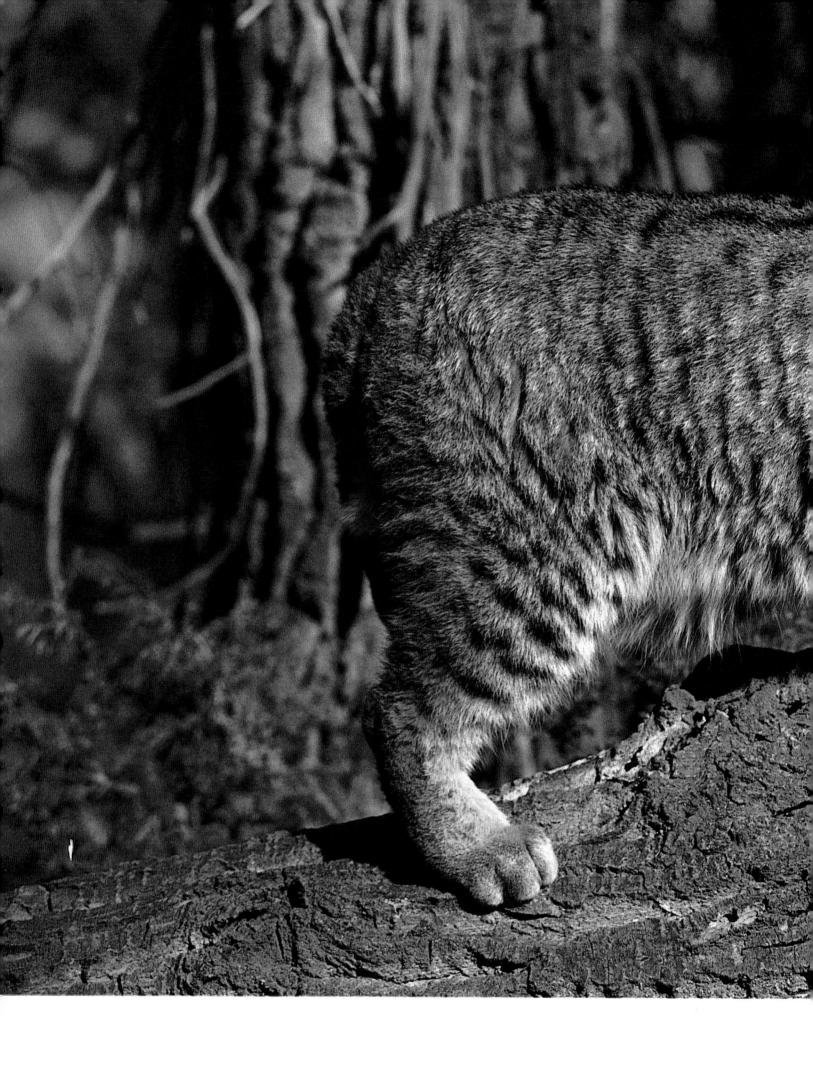

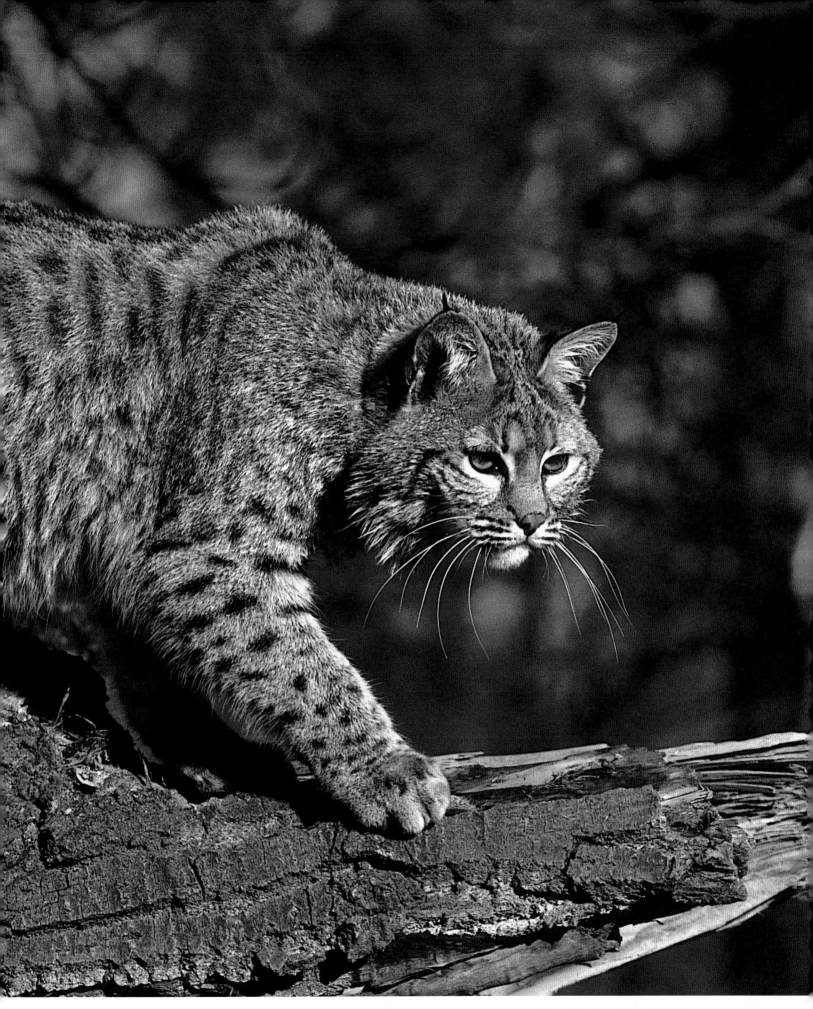

Just like domestic cats, lynx and bobcats communicate their moods through a subtle and expressive vocabulary of body positions. With its tucked-in tail and crouched stance, this bobcat registers mild fear. If it were terrified or ready to submit, it would lower its body to the ground and fold its ears down flat. Tom Walker

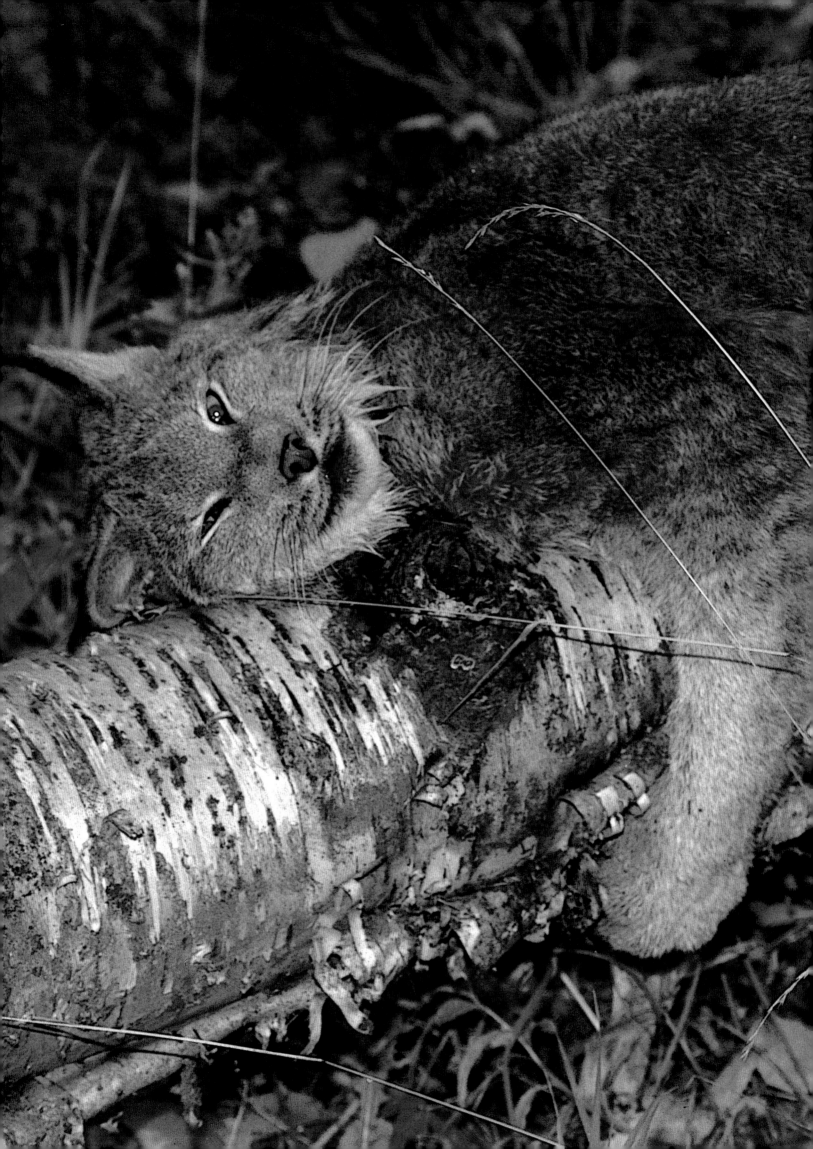

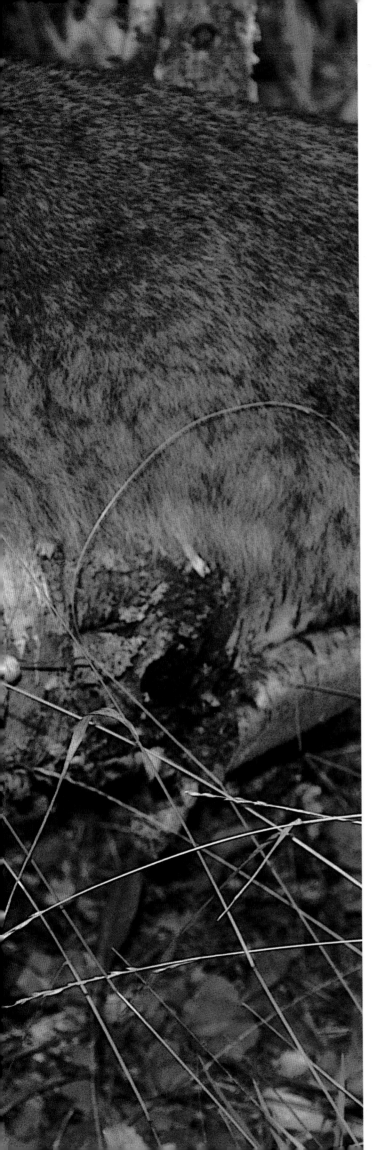

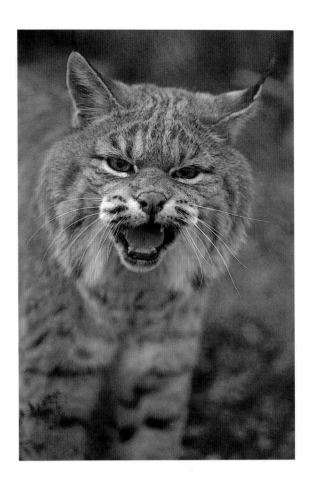

Mrrow! *This bobcat signals an angry or aggressive mood by standing tall, holding its ears upright and twisting them around so that the backs are visible. This posture means "Get lost!" in cat parlance.* Dennis W. Schmidt/Valan Photos

Left: *A lynx rubs its head and neck on a log, leaving a trace of its body scent to advertise its presence. Wild cats often rub their heads against their own urine marks, creating an olfactory link between themselves and their hunting grounds.* Erwin & Peggy Bauer

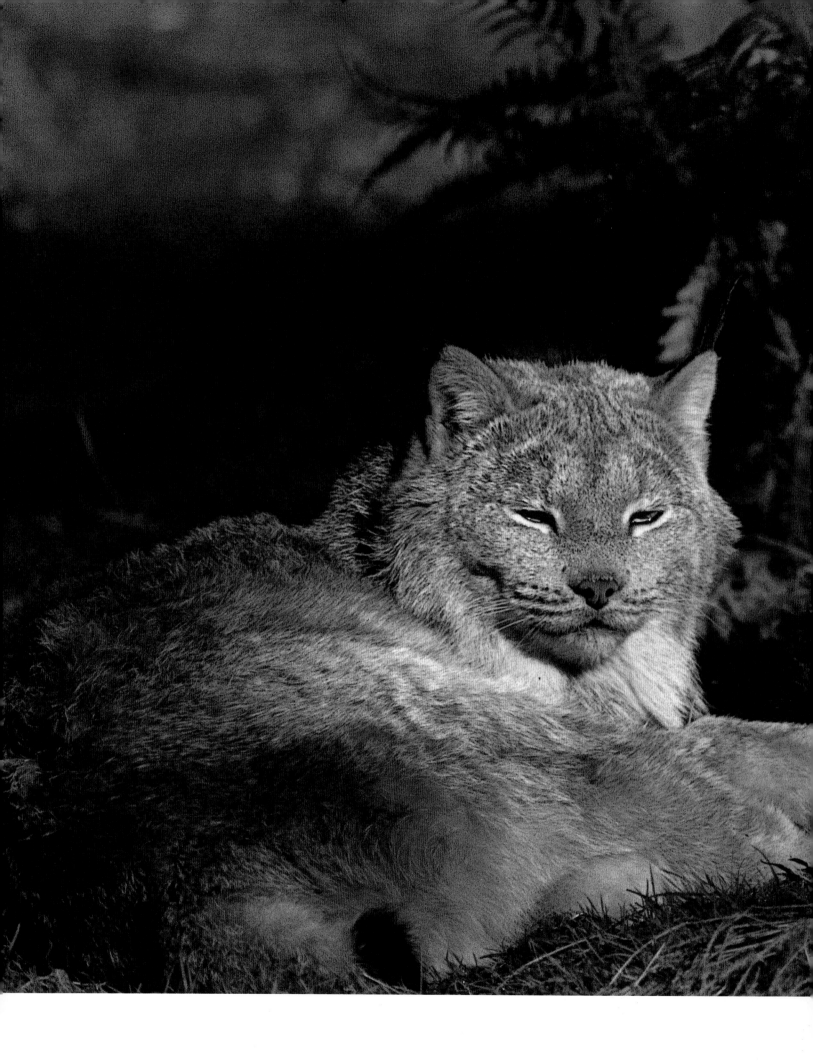

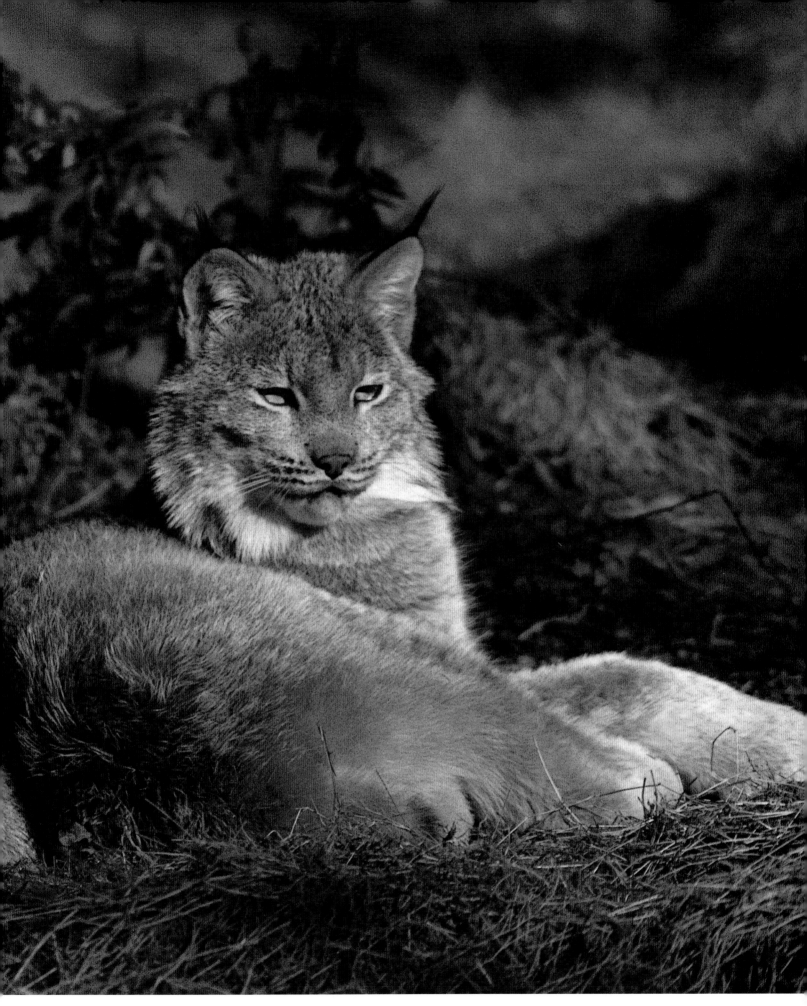

The home range of an adult male lynx or bobcat always overlaps the living space of one or more adult females. The sexes get together for a few days each year when the female is ready to breed—a condition she signals through her scent marks and lewd caterwauling. Although this couple looks very peaceful, mating cats usually indulge in a wild rumpus of chasing, biting and fevered copulation. Tom & Pat Leeson

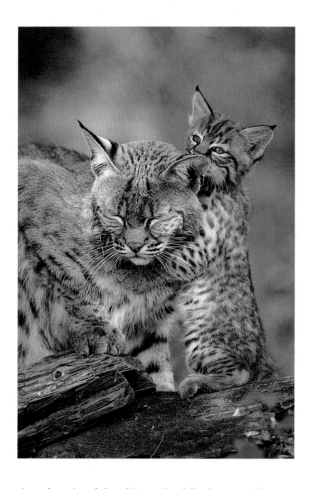

A rambunctious bobcat kitten takes full advantage of its mother's patience. Art Wolfe

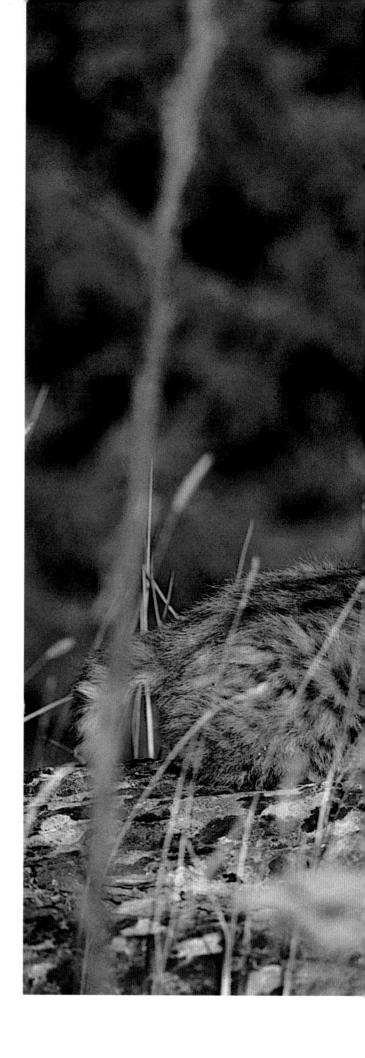

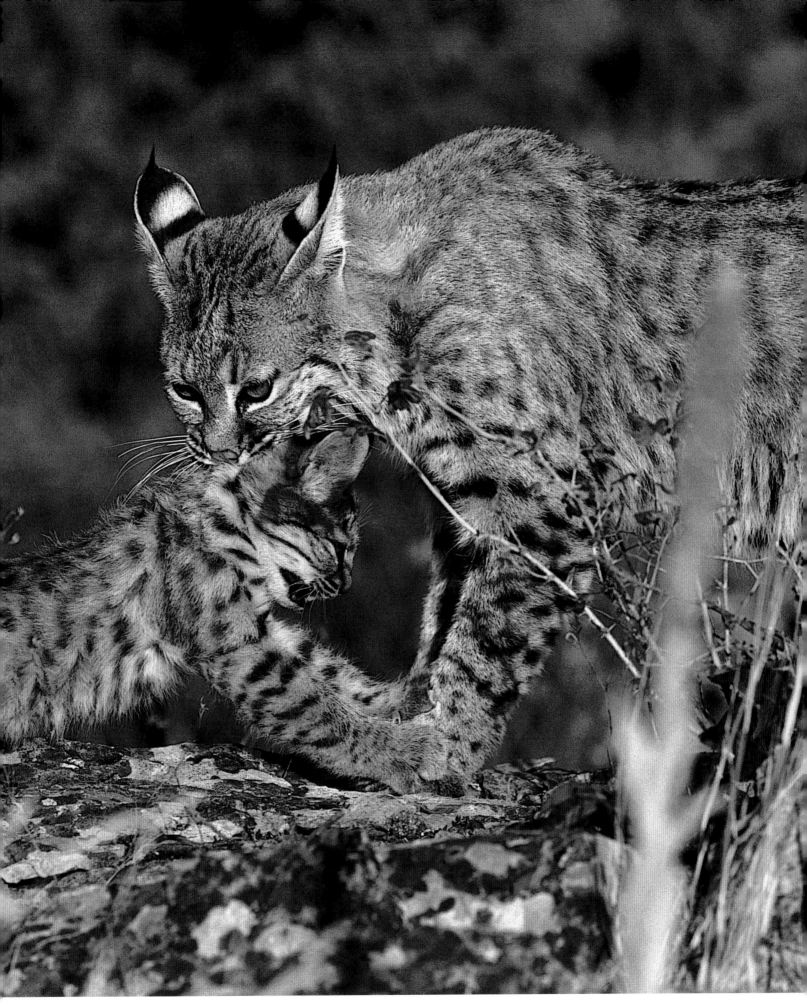

A mother bobcat struggles to transport a protesting kitten. Bobcats and lynx usually mate in the late winter (often in February or March), and the young are born about nine weeks later, into the welcoming spring warmth. Alan & Sandy Carey

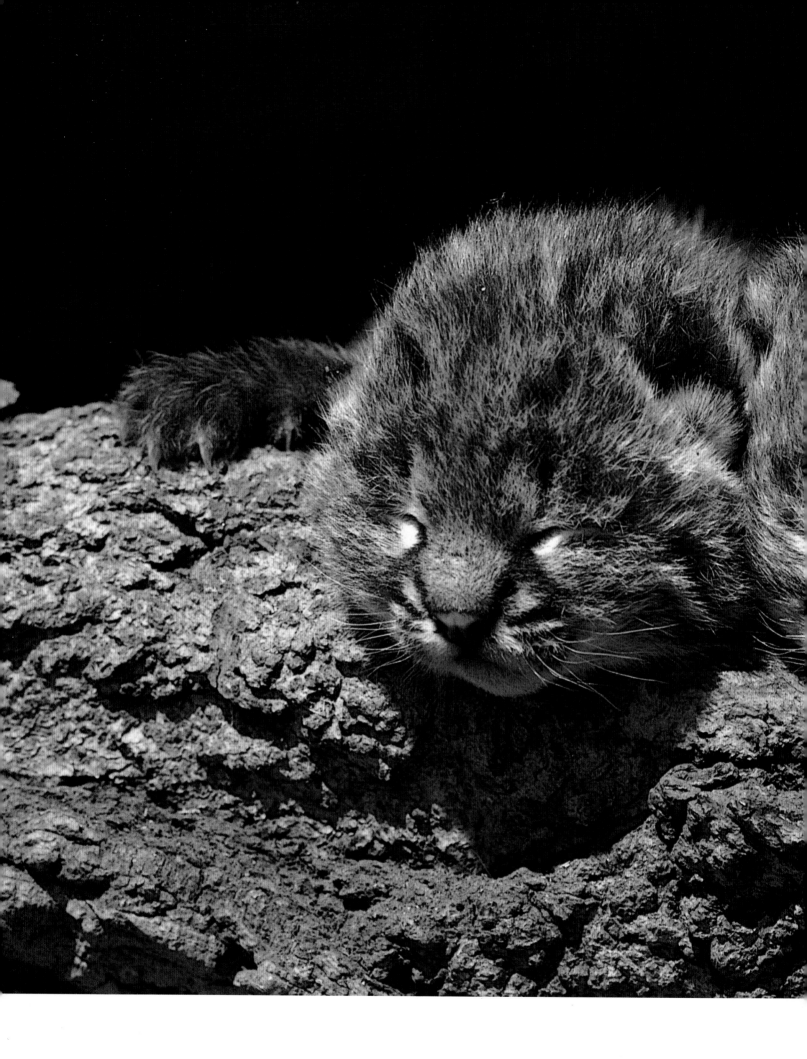

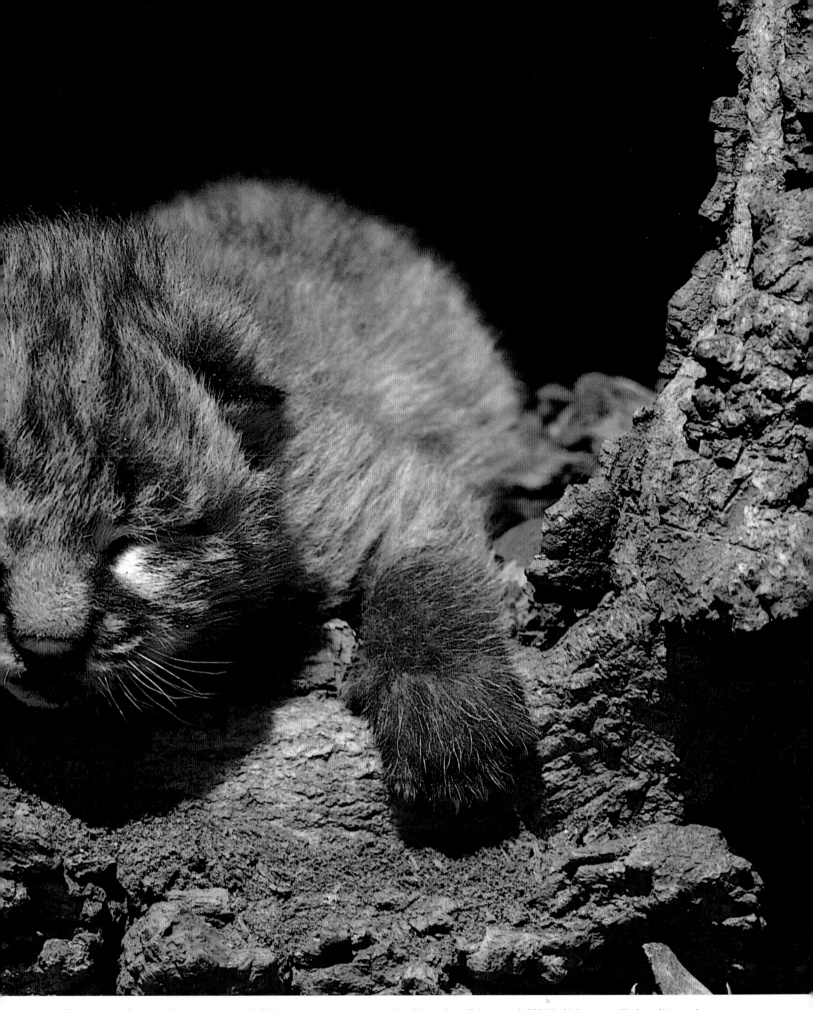

Their eyes and ears still closed, two week-old bobcats snooze at the mouth of their den. Bobcats and Old World lynx usually bear litters of two or three, while North American lynx average three or four kittens. Leonard Lee Rue III

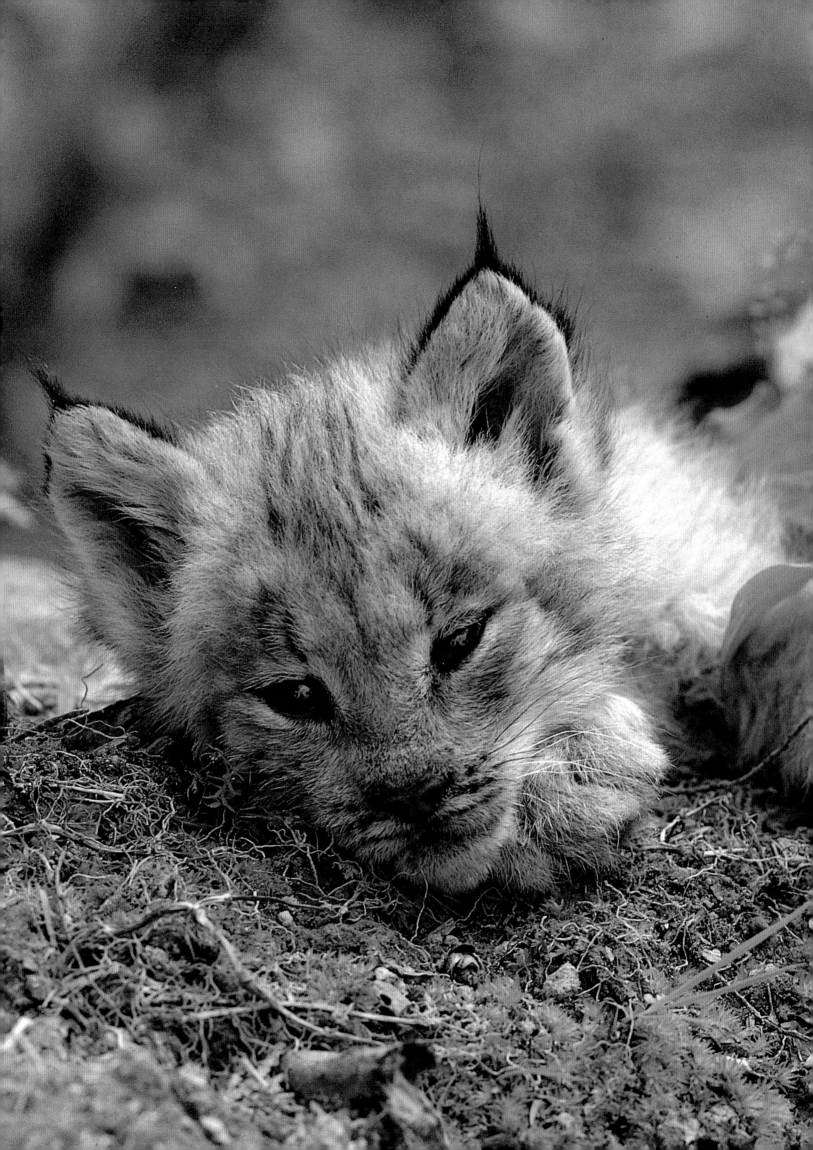

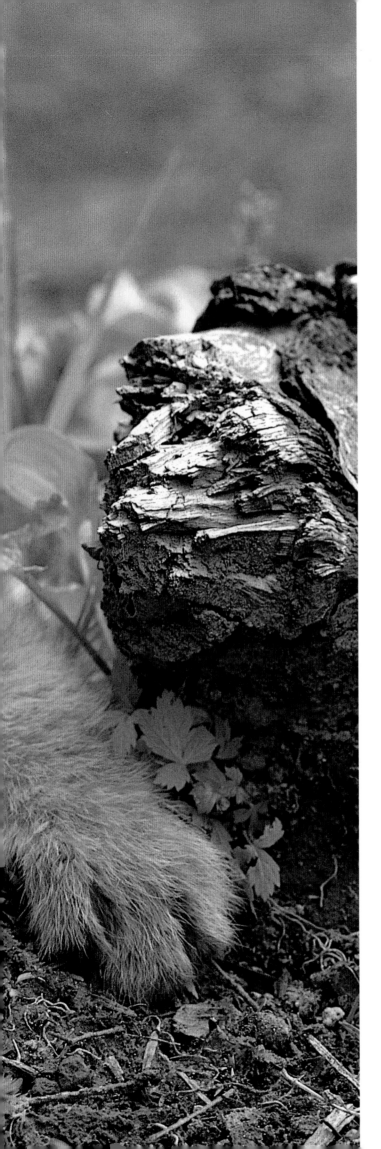

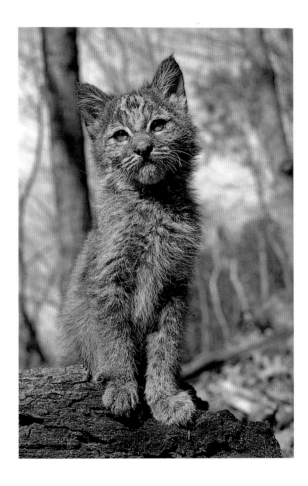

A three-month-old bobcat takes time out from rough-housing to pose for a portrait. Leonard Lee Rue III

Left: *Its long ear tufts already apparent, a soft-furred lynx kit snuggles into the moss. If one of its family members approached, the kitten might purr in greeting.* Murray O'Neill/Valan Photos

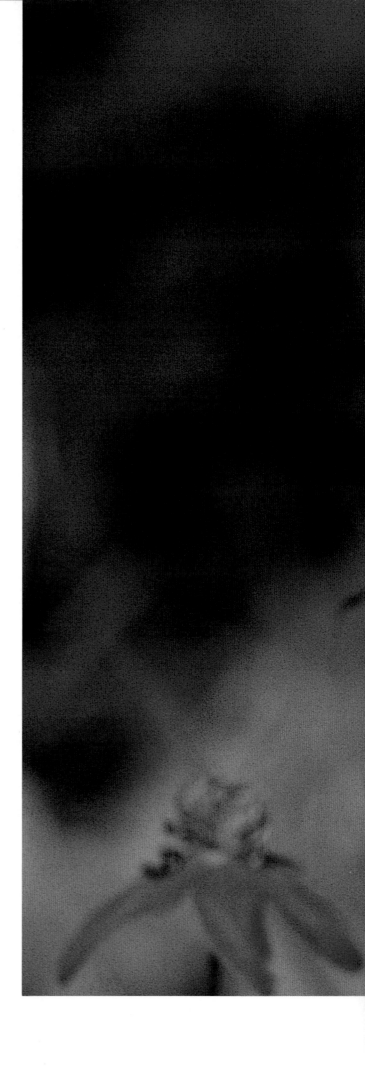

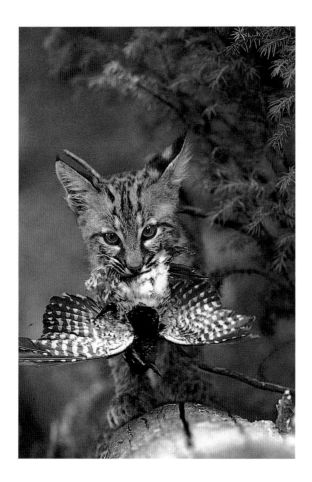

In the year they spend with their mothers, lynx and bobcat kittens progress from cuddly helplessness to self-sufficiency. Long before they can hunt for themselves, the kittens hone their skills by playing with prey that their mother brings in. This young bobcat has a firm grip on a yellow-bellied sapsucker. Erwin & Peggy Bauer

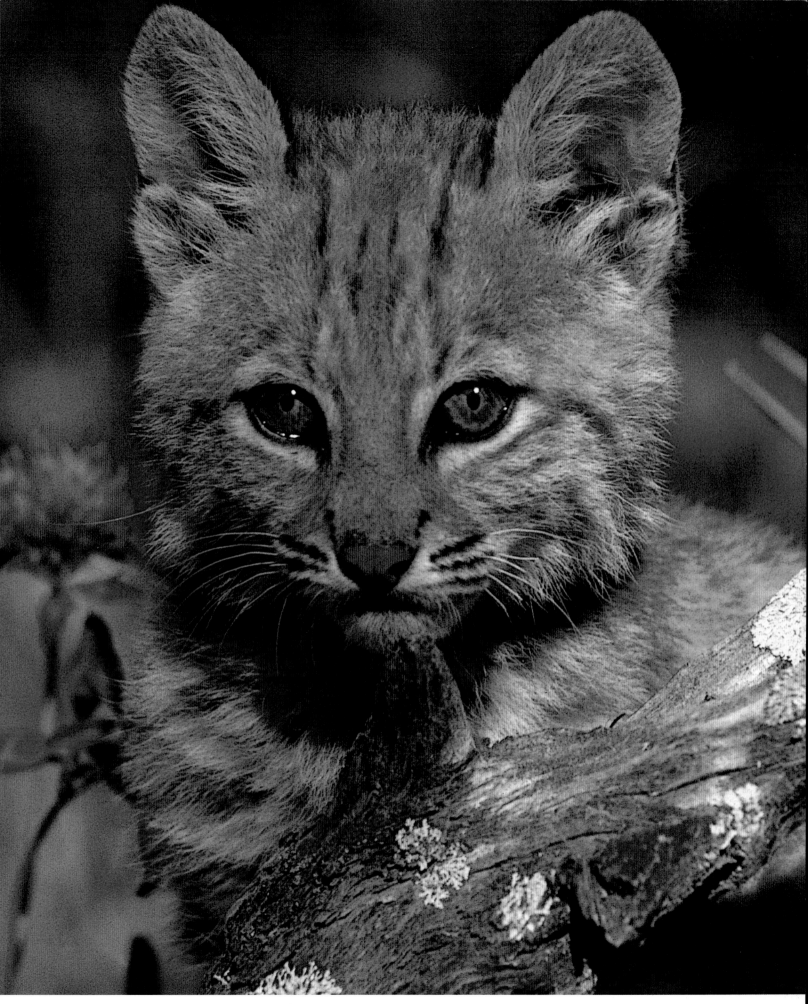

Framed by clover and fireweed, a young bobcat explores the world around its den. Erwin & Peggy Bauer

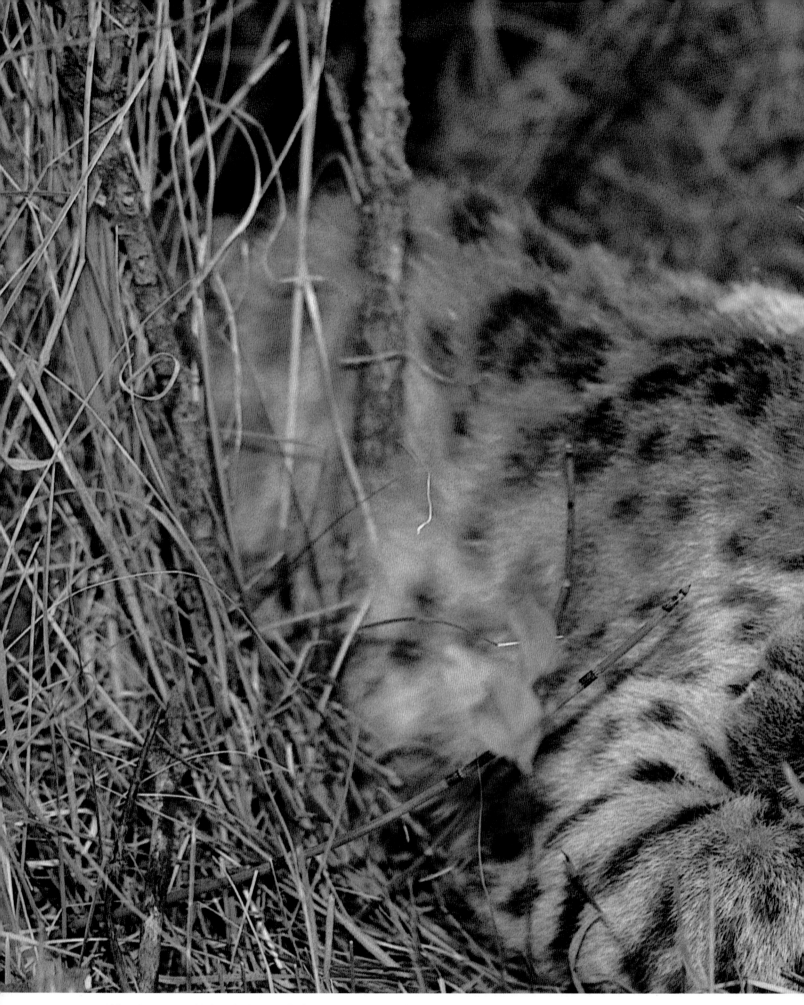

Although no one is likely to be hurt in the kittens' tussling, play fights do have a serious aspect. They are the school in which young cats develop the strength and agility they will require as solitary hunters. Victoria Hurst

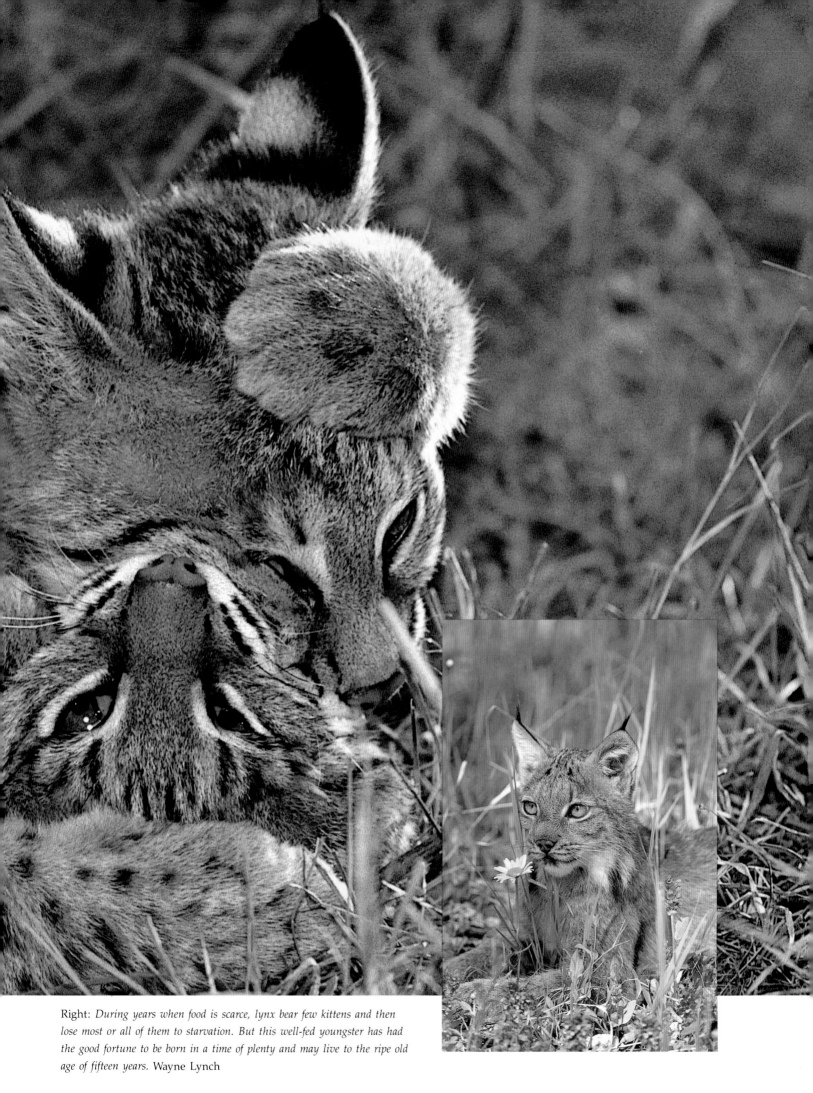

Right: *During years when food is scarce, lynx bear few kittens and then lose most or all of them to starvation. But this well-fed youngster has had the good fortune to be born in a time of plenty and may live to the ripe old age of fifteen years.* Wayne Lynch

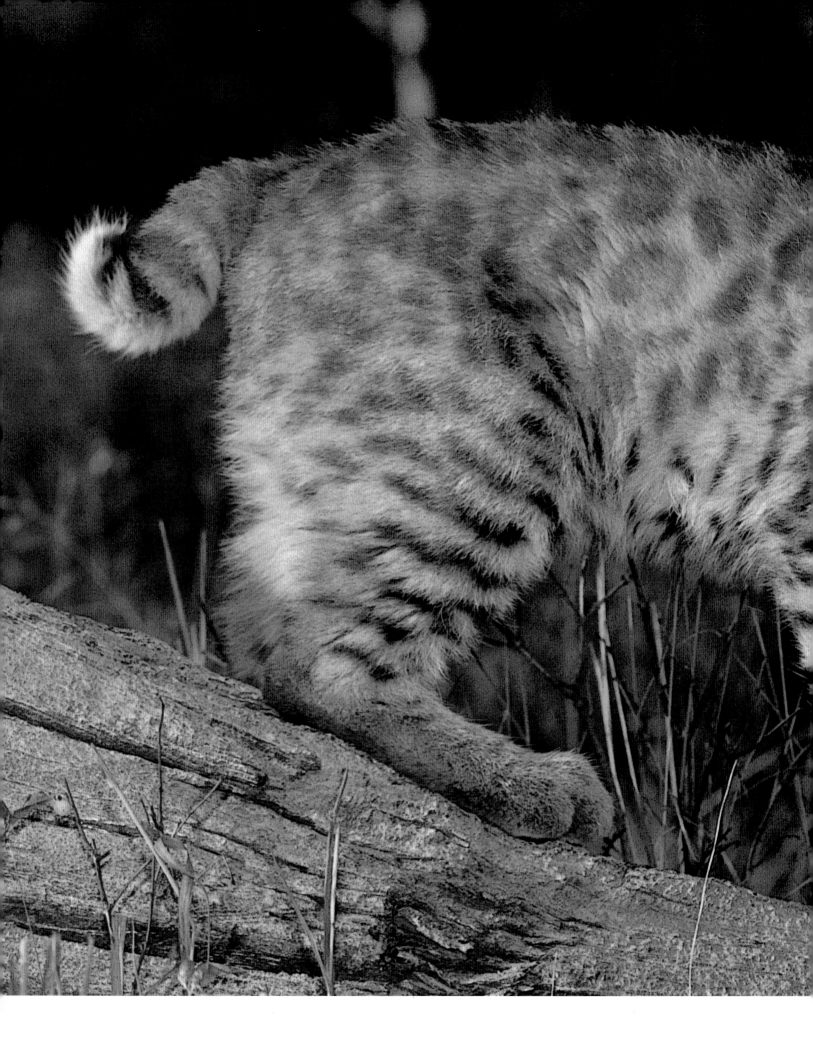

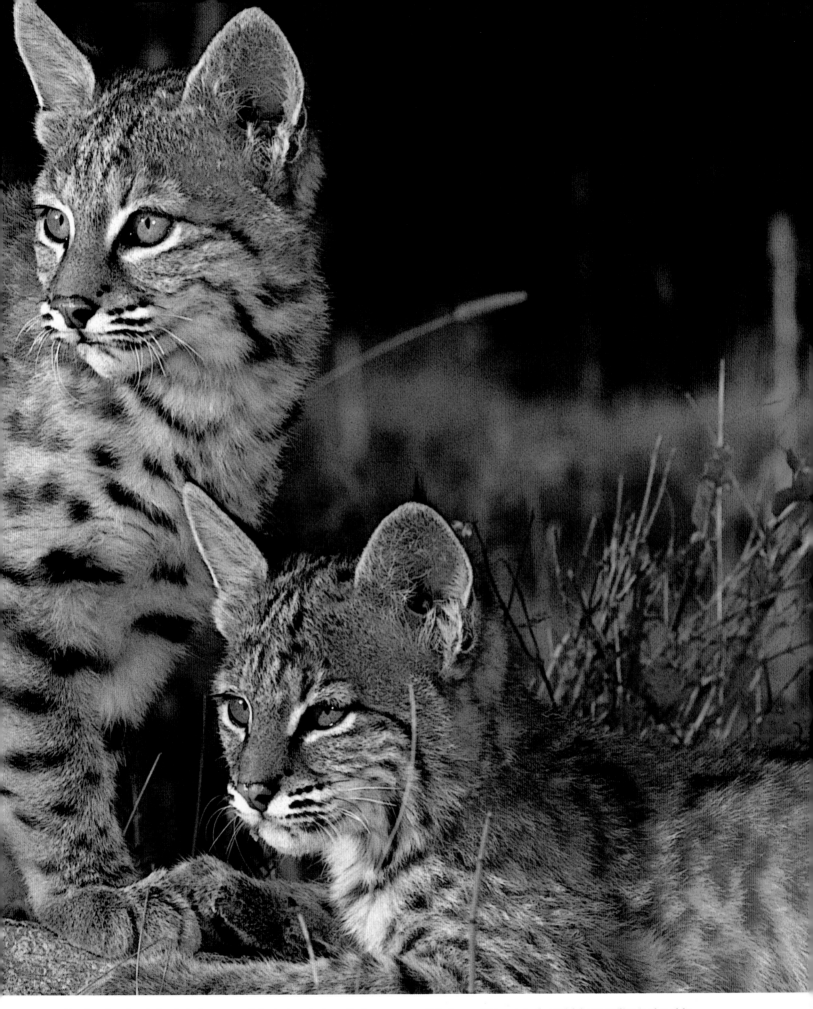

Keenly relaxed, calmly alert, two young bobcats turn to investigate an unseen disturbance. This spirit of watchful tranquility is shared by the whole cat tribe. Victoria Hurst

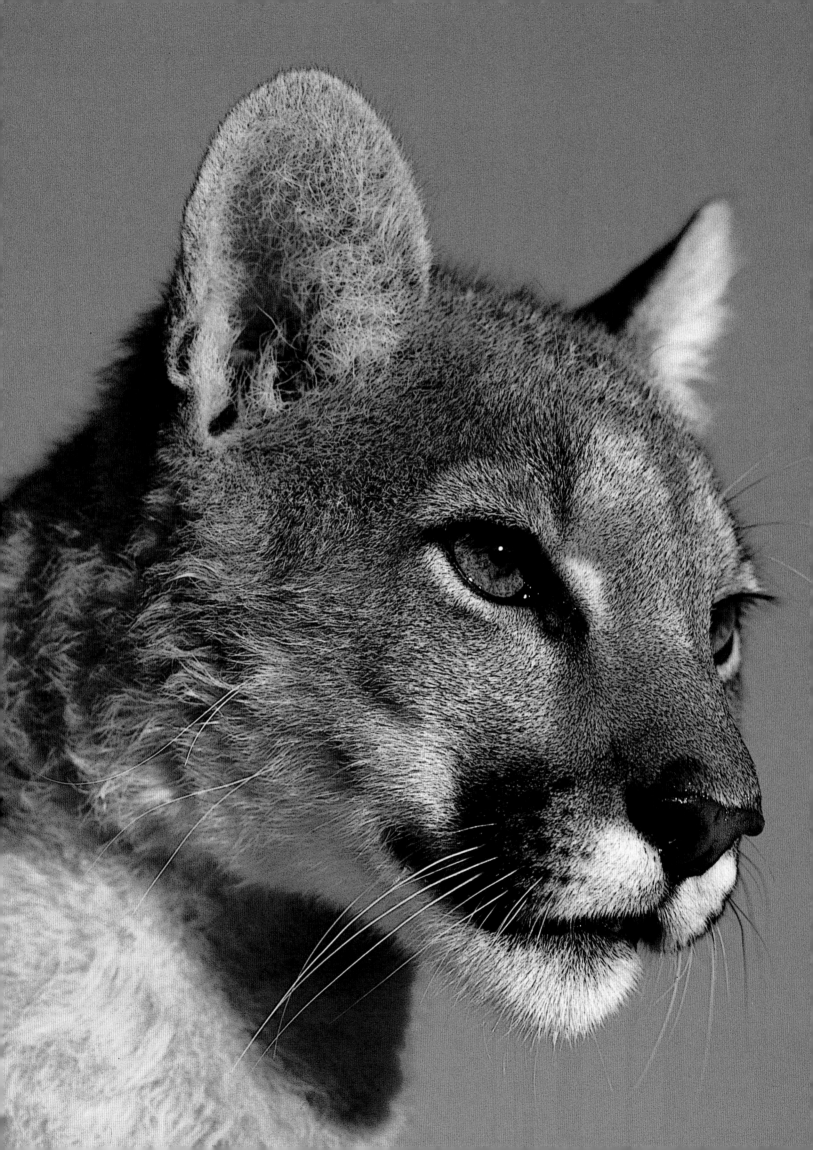

MOUNTAIN LIONS

"LET US REMEMBER THAT [THE MOUNTAIN
LION] IS IN ALL PHYSICAL RESPECTS
A CAT, SIMPLY A CAT MULTIPLED BY 20."

—Ernest Thompson Seton,
Lives of Game Animals

Beep. Beep. Beep.

With his left hand, biologist Martin Jalkotzy lifts the small boxlike radio receiver to his ear, trying to make the most of the faint squawks that it emits. With his right, he holds up what looks like an old-fashioned TV antenna and turns it through a jerky circuit. North, north-west, west...

We are standing at the edge of a paved highway, looking out over the broad dark-green sweep of the Sheep River Valley in western Alberta. During the summer, this road is arush with cars of holiday-makers, many from nearby Calgary, who come to test themselves against the slopes of the Rocky Mountain foothills. But now, in late winter, the road is closed to regular traffic, and the valley is hushed.

Beep. Beep. Beep.

Martin is still listening, chin slightly raised, eyes half shut. After several days as a guest of the Alberta Cougar Project, I know better than to interrupt him. Pinpointing signals from a radio-collared animal is less a science than an art, and Martin deserves his concentration. Besides, if he succeeds, I might get to see a wild mountain lion. I do my best to appear patient.

Beep. Beep.

Young mountain lion. *Denver Bryan*

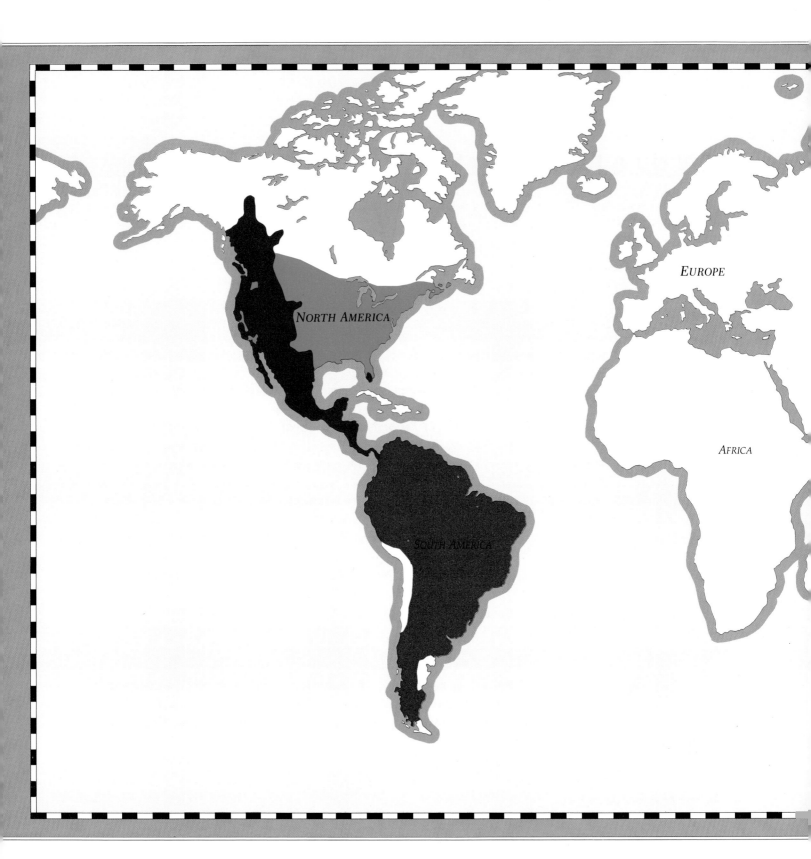

EUROPE

AFRICA

NORTH AMERICA

SOUTH AMERICA

Current and historic distributions for North America are based on information published in the July 1992 issue of *National Geographic*. The range for South America comes from *Great Cats: Majestic Creatures of the Wild* by John Seidensticker and Susan Lumpkin, Rodale Press, 1991.

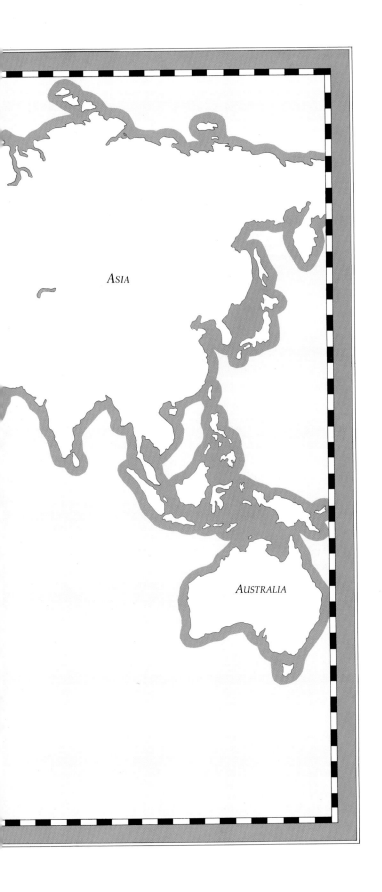

PRESENT AND HISTORIC DISTRIBUTION
OF THE MOUNTAIN LION

PRESENT RANGE

HISTORIC RANGE (information available
for North America only)

Finally Martin lowers the receiver from his ear. "I think it's coming from up there," he says, jerking his head to indicate the gentle slope behind us. "She might be quite close." "She" is the source of the signals: an adult female mountain lion nicknamed Geisha, who for the past eight years has unwittingly sent out telltale beeps from a small radio transmitter that she wears under her chin. Guided by these insistent monotone messages, Martin and his colleagues have been able to gather information about her diet, movements and sexual encounters. They know, for example, that early last fall she gave birth to two fluffy blue-eyed kittens. Are her youngsters with her now? There is only one way to find out.

We turn our backs to the road and follow a streambed through a border of meadows and open woods. If it weren't for Martin's frequent stops to consult his equipment, this walk would be no different from dozens of other afternoon rambles through the foothills. Overhead the sun breaks through fitfully; underfoot the snow and dry leaves crunch.

We have walked for about ten minutes when Martin, again checking his receiver, whispers "This way" and makes a sharp right turn into the woods. The trees stand in clumps, with leads of open space that take us in like paths. It is so easy and so ordinary that I cannot believe anything exciting will happen.

Then it does. A burnished beige blur streaks out of a grove of willows and spruce, half a minute ahead. While I am trying to figure out what it was and where it went, Martin points towards the thicket. More brown shapes are moving in the darkness under the branches of a large spruce. As the animals shift around to get

Felis concolor, *the cat of one colour, might unofficially be dubbed* Felis polynomen, *the cat of many names. In the eastern United States, including Florida, the species is known as the ''panther'' (or, rarely, ''painter''), a misidentification that has been held over from colonial times. Elsewhere in the U.S., it is known either as the ''puma,'' a name contributed by the Incas of Peru, or ''cougar,'' a word that comes from Brazil. ''Cougar'' is also the name that is commonly heard amongst Canadians. One term that may have a broader currency is ''mountain lion,'' and I have adopted it in a spirit of compromise, although our ''lions'' are not confined to the mountains and have little in common with their African and Asian namesakes.*

a look at us, we catch the flash of their amber eyes and brilliant white muzzles. Mountain lions.

A few minutes of utter silence. Then Martin motions me closer, leans back against a tree and begins to offer a muttered commentary. The animals in the thicket are—

"Look, look, look," I sputter. Without a rustle of notice, one of the mountain lions has positioned itself in front of the spruce tree. It faces us head on, its big round eyes fixed on us like laser beams. We are all motionless. Then the animal bounds towards us, closing the space. At two-seconds' distance it stops and eyes us intently again.

Beside its back right heel, the tip of its tail ticks.

"It's okay," Martin whispers. "It's just curious." Sure enough, this is no snarling, ears-back, mad-cat attack. Instead the animal looks incredulous, as if confronted by aliens from outer space. Its unblinking round-eyed stare never wavers. It bounces closer.

Martin takes a step forward. The cat turns away; another step from Martin and it scoots back to the safety of the thicket. Martin and I turn as well and walk back to the road.

About the time I start breathing again, I realize that Martin is trying to fill me in on what has happened. The animal who came towards us was one of Geisha's half-grown kittens, a youngster who did not know enough to avoid humans. The mother, being more experienced, had streaked away in the first instant. She may still be in the area, waiting for us to leave. Or maybe she has taken advantage of the disturbance to head off for several days of hunting. When she makes a kill, she will come back and collect her kittens.

I cannot believe my good luck. Nobody gets to see a wild mountain lion. Even researchers like Martin are limited to an occasional fleeting glance. And to see one in this familiar landscape, so close to a paved road. How many times have I walked or driven past a mountain lion and never realized it?

Apparently I am not alone in my ignorance. When Martin tells people about his research, they usually look askance. "You mean there are still mountain lions out there?" they ask. "Then they must be endangered." But whether we notice them or not, the cats are definitely there—some twenty thousand in North America. Still the most widely distributed land mammal in the western hemisphere (apart from ourselves), mountain lions range across western Canada and the western U.S., through foothills, mountains and canyon country, rainforest, mixed woods and chaparral. They even lick out into the Canadian prairies, by following treed river valleys into deepest Saskatchewan and Manitoba. In many western states, where grizzlies and wolves have long since been driven into extinction, mountain lions survive as the only large predators.

From the U.S.-Mexico border south, the cats make their homes in mountains, forests, grasslands and swamps all the way to land's end in Patagonia. Nobody has a clue how many mountain lions exist in Central and South America, nor how they are coping with the human assault on tropical ecosystems.

Despite these large unknowns, it is fair to state that mountain lions are not endangered, taken as a whole. In other words, they are not on their deathbed as a species. At the same time, they are clearly neither as numerous nor as widespread as they were quite recently. Within the past 150 years, North American lions (which are now confined to the western third of the continent) ranged eastward to the Atlantic coast. According to one early writer, a Colonel H. W. Shoemaker, "The woods [of Pennsylvania] teemed with them.... Almost every backwoods kitchen had a Panther [mountain lion] coverlet on the lounge by the stove. Panther tracks could be seen crossing and re-crossing all the fields, yet children on their way to school were never molested."

Although the colonel had many seconders among frontier-folk for his report of the "panther's" abundance, he was not typical in his assessment of its nature. Around 1700, an Englishman named John Lawson opined (on

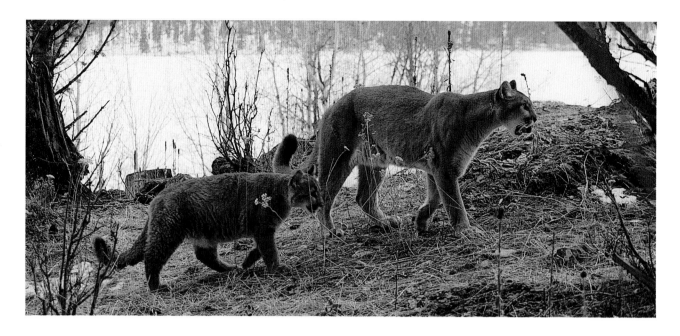

A female mountain lion and her kitten stroll through an open forest. *Kent & Donna Dannen*

what basis we do not know) that "This beast is the greatest Enemy of the Planter, of any Vermine in Carolina." Other Carolinans fed their taste for horror by recounting tales of yowling male panthers that preyed on pregnant women. Far and wide, the lion was feared as a man-killer and reviled for stealing game and livestock from innocent settlers. Even sometime-conservationist Theodore Roosevelt blasted "the big horse-killing cat, the destroyer of the deer, the lord of stealthy murder, . . . [that faces] his doom with a heart both craven and cruel."

Judging from present-day experience, these statements were and are grotesque misrepresentations. True, mountain lions do occasionally attack people, particularly small children, but these calamities tend to be localized (Vancouver Island and some parts of California are current hot spots) and are also exceptionally rare. In the past hundred years, there have been nine documented human fatalities, making it a thousand times more likely that you will be killed by lightning than by a mountain lion. And though it is true that mountain lions can learn to kill cattle and other livestock, few of them actually do. An individual sheep-eating lion can cause

big problems for a small rancher (problems the cat will likely pay for with its life), but a typical population of wild cats will never pose a significant threat to the livestock industry. As to the complaint that mountain lions steal food from the mouths of human hunters, it is hard to take such statements seriously, given the balance of power that now exists between the two species.

Belief justifies action, and the belief in a demonic, despicable panther justified an all-out assault on it. Colonel Shoemaker recounts with grief the exploits of a Black Jack Schwartz who, in 1760, rallied his friends and neighbours in Snyder County, Pennsylvania, to hold a ring hunt, or animal drive. Killed within a 25-kilometre (15-mile) radius were "41 Panthers, 109 Wolves, 112 Foxes, 114 Mountain Cats, 17 Black Bears, 1 White Bear, 2 Elk, 98 Deer, 111 Buffaloes, 3 Fishers, 1 Otter, 12 Gluttons [Wolverines], 3 Beavers, and upwards of 500 smaller animals."

Pennsylvania's final ring hunt was held in 1849. In the meantime, "panthers," "pumas," "cougars," "mountain cats" and "lions" had been put under bounty in that state and across the continent. California went so far as to employ professional lion hunters, with the result that an estimated 12,500 mountain lions were killed within its boundaries between 1907 and 1963. Apparently the work paid off in personal satisfaction as well as in cash. "Anybody can kill a deer," observed Ben Lilly, one of California's salaried hunters. "It takes a man to kill a varmint." The manly toil of extermination persisted until 1970, when the last of the bounties was finally cancelled.

Add to this assault the clearing of the eastern forests to create farmland, and the fate of the mountain lion was decided in eastern North America. In subsequent years, many of the hard-won farms have been abandoned and reclaimed by the forest, but though the trees have returned and the deer have returned, the mountain lions have not.

Or—just maybe—a very few have. Maybe they weren't completely wiped out after all. In 1938, several decades after the eastern population was thought to be extinct, a mountain lion was killed in northern Maine, its body stuffed and taken to the University of New Brunswick in Fredericton. This aging artifact is the last concrete proof that *Felis concolor couguar*, the eastern subspecies, might have managed to hang on. Ever since, there's been a persistent buzz of reports that the cats are still with us. Every year dozens of hunters, fishermen, wildlife officers and others come out of the forests of Ontario, Michigan, Atlantic Canada, New England, Pennsylvania, the Virginias, the Carolinas and Georgia to certify, in tones of bug-eyed amazement, that they have seen a mountain lion. Most such reports are mistaken—like the man who killed a black panther that turned out to be a house cat—but some come from qualified people and are probably accurate.

Unfortunately, a file of "probably accurate" reports does not constitute proof. And all recent attempts to produce verification, including a five-year-long study in the southern Appalachians, have come up empty-handed. Does this mean that the cats are not there or simply that they have avoided detection? Is the eastern subspecies still around? To date, the answer is a firm, well-researched "perhaps."

The only population of mountain lions that *is* known to survive east of the Mississippi is the Florida panther, *Felis concolor coryi*. Since its existence was demonstrated in 1973—there's nothing like a live-caught cat to set the doubts to rest—Florida's panther population has been estimated at between thirty and fifty animals. In the opinion of experts with the state's game commission, they exhibit "symptoms of a slow and rather certain extinction process." Specifically, many of them suffer from poor nutrition, because their habitat is declining in both area and quality. The cats also show signs of severe inbreeding, caused by their low numbers and by the intrusions of industrial society, which divide the population into ever smaller disconnected fragments. Several of the identifying characteristics of the Florida subspecies, such as a sharp crook at the end of the tail, have recently been diagnosed as genetic defects. Parasites and serious diseases are widespread; the number of kittens that survive in some areas is extremely low; and almost all the sperm produced by the males are abnormal.

The good people of Florida have answered the call. Studies have been funded. Nature preserves and wildlife refuges have been enlarged. Deer hunting has been restricted. Speed limits have been posted in critical areas to reduce road-kills. Millions of dollars have been spent on thirty-six wildlife underpasses to provide safe crossings of Alligator Alley, the four-lane interstate that rips through Fakahatchee Strand.

And even bigger challenges lie just ahead. One is to protect panther habitat on privately owned lands, an undertaking that could gobble up billions of taxpayers' dollars in compensation payments. The other is to roughly triple the number of panthers by breeding them in captivity. This will involve catching kittens (about half of which die in the wild), shipping them to zoos and other facilities (where more of them will survive), breeding them by artificial insemination and shipping their offspring back to south Florida's swampy countryside. Unless this complex intervention succeeds, computer projections predict that the Florida panther—despite everything else that has been accomplished on its behalf—will disappear by the year 2015.

Once an animal becomes endangered, it may be lucky enough to get intensive care, with round-the-clock, high-tech surveillance and a huge expenditure of cash and effort. Even so, it clings to life by a thread. As Charles Darwin once put it, "Rarity is the precursor to extinction," and often there is not much we can do to slow or stop the process. But what we can do, with only a moderate outlay and almost certain success, is to protect healthy populations where the animals are still normally abundant and vigorous. In the case of the mountain lion, good health now lies out west.

By all recent standards, western populations seem to be plentiful. In the past twenty-odd years, they may have increased about four-fold, thanks to the elimination of bounties and removal of the species from the "varmint" category. In most western jurisdictions, mountain lions are now listed as "game animals," a classification that, with variably sized loopholes for predator "control," permits the number of killings to be limited through a licensing system. The desk work has been well done.

But the grunt work—getting out into mountain-lion country, tracking down the cats, counting their kittens to study their rate of reproduction, walking in on kills to learn about their diet, trying by fair means or foul to estimate the local population, establishing "safe" levels of hunting, studying the effects of various methods of logging, and doing it over and over, year after year, in different localities—has not received the same public endorsement. As a result, there are still many populations about which we are ignorant. "The attitude seems to be, if it's not broken, don't fix it," says wild-cat expert Maurice Hornocker who, in the late 1960s, became one of the first people to radio-collar and study wild mountain lions. "Because of tight-fisted funding, unless animals are in trouble, they don't get any attention."

The Sheep River study is one of a handful that are currently underway in Canada and the United States. Although it receives logistical support from government (for example, the use of a house and assorted "trikes" and "quads" for travelling back-country trails), it relies for money on a precarious alliance of private sponsors. In the final analysis, what keeps it going is the bone-deep dedication of Martin Jalkotzy and his two partners, Ian Ross and Ralph Schmidt. No day is too long, no hillside too steep, no trail too footsore. They carry on carrying on, unstoppable as androids.

The morning after the encounter with Geisha and her kittens, Ian is up, dressed, fed, loaded with equipment and on the trail by 7:05. The rest of us, including two hounds named Buford and Zed, are not far behind. We spend the morning labouring through the chop of hills, sweating up steep cutlines, pausing on each likely ridge to check for guiding beeps, then plunging headlong into the next valley. Upslope and down, Buford and Zed strain at the ends of their leads. When the cutlines end, we scramble through underbrush, over fallen logs, sliding in fresh snow. On the ascents my thighs are leaden; on the descents my kneecaps burn. Always ahead, at the edge of my field of vision, the researchers press on.

The object of their quest is a male mountain lion dubbed Thor, whose radio collar is overdue for replacement. He had not been heard from for several weeks—had the batteries that powered his transmitter already gone dead?—but yesterday he was back again, loud and clear on the radio dial. It seems he had been off exploring the frontiers of his large home range—some 300 square kilometres (115 square miles)—until urgent business called him back into radio contact. That urgent business was a female cat named Quick. Over the past several weeks, the researchers had noticed that Quick was no longer travelling with her two year-old kittens, a probable sign that she was ready to breed. Thor's timely reappearance turned that conjecture into a certainty, especially when their tracks were seen together, his as broad as an adult's hand, hers looking kittenish by comparison. Now their signals are coming from the same valley, somewhere ahead.

At the top of a small mountain, I pause to catch my breath. Behind me, in the distance, the landscape folds up on itself in misty innocence.

Below, I can hear Buford and Zed baying on fresh scent, a sound that prickles the back of my neck. I head towards it.

By the time I get there, the chase is over. The howling dogs are tied around the margins of a small clearing, facing a grove of large pines, and on a broad branch overhead lies Thor, treed by some ancestral fear of baying predators. With the hullabaloo safely below him, he seems to be calm and relaxed. A heavily muscled forelimb dangles down from the branch. He looks like a burly tomcat sprawled on a giant chairback. His gaze, when he turns towards me, is piercingly direct.

From then on it is clockwork: a tranquillizing dart slaps into his hip, his body goes limp, and he is dangled with ropes to the ground. The researchers stretch him out carefully and bend over him, changing his collar, checking his teeth and claws, taking measurements. On the ground he looks small; the scale shows his weight as 60 kilograms (about 130 pounds). Not much for an animal that makes his living by killing, unaided, moose calves that are more than three times his size.

When the researchers have finished their tasks, we stand back and wait for Thor to come around. For a time the only motion is the gentle in-and-out of his breath. Then he lifts his head languorously, lets it drop, lifts it again, struggles to his feet and stumbles off into the forest.

I think of Quick who is out there, too, and of the two youngsters who are beginning to take up the challenges of adult life. And, of course, I remember the other young cat, the one with the searching eyes. Wordlessly, I wish them good luck and turn my thoughts towards home.

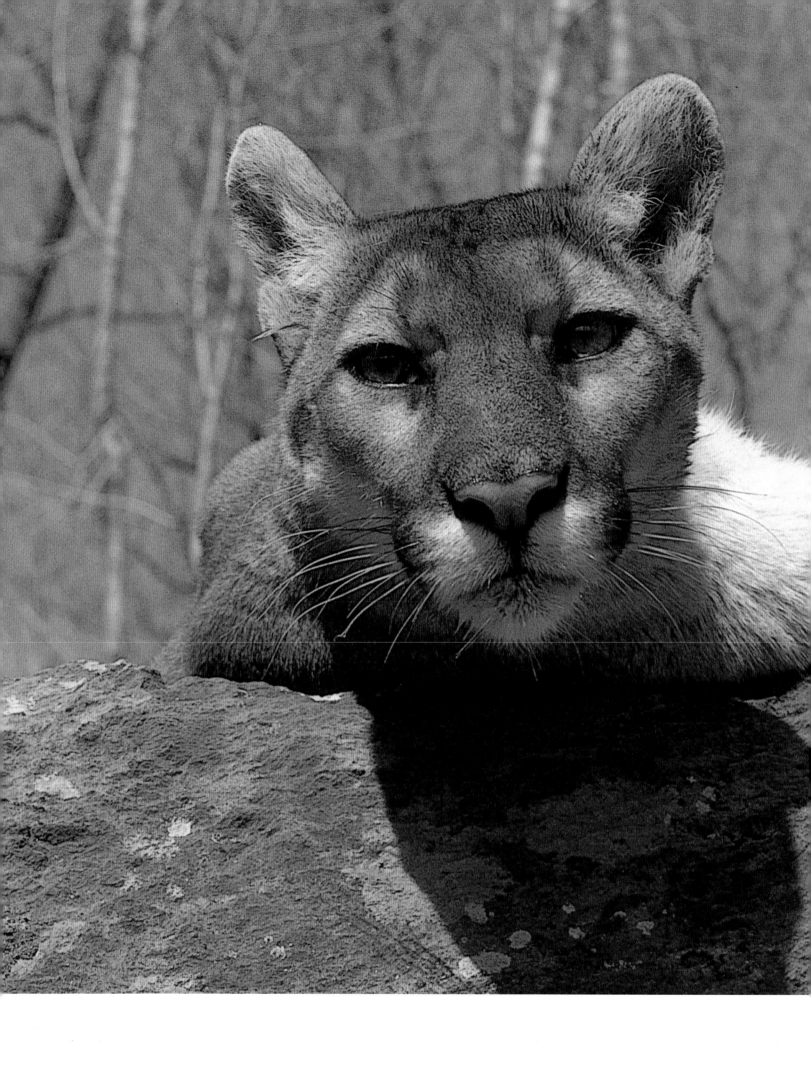

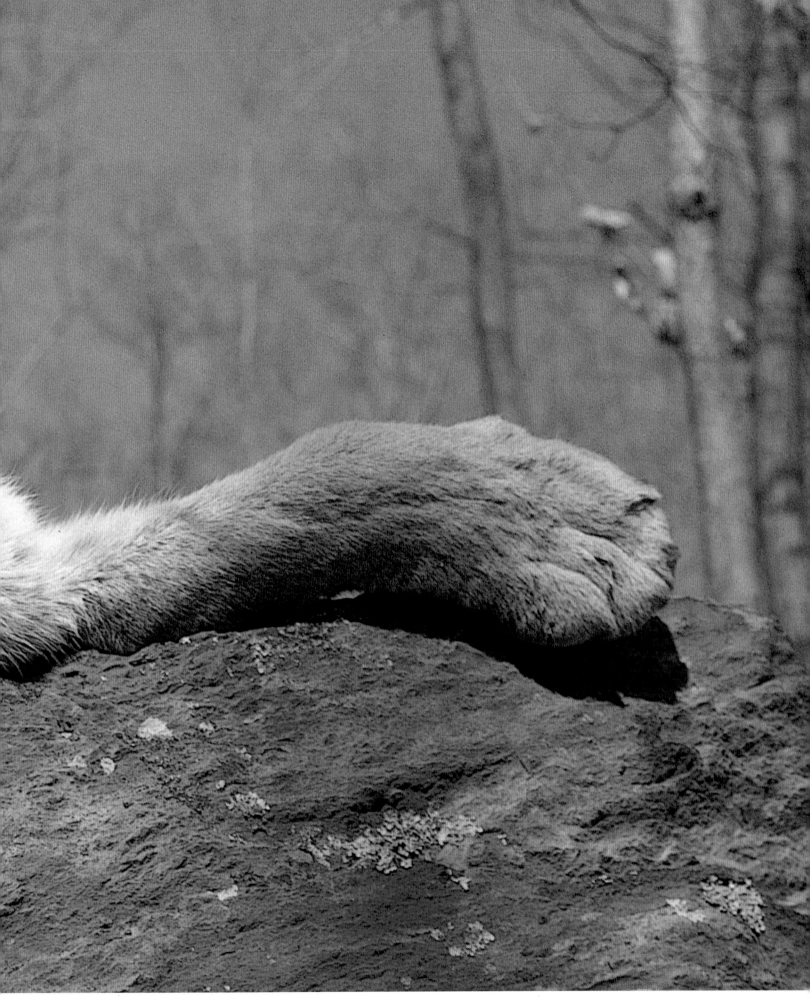

With an intensity of focus that is pure cat, a mountain lion stretches across a boulder. Leonard Lee Rue III

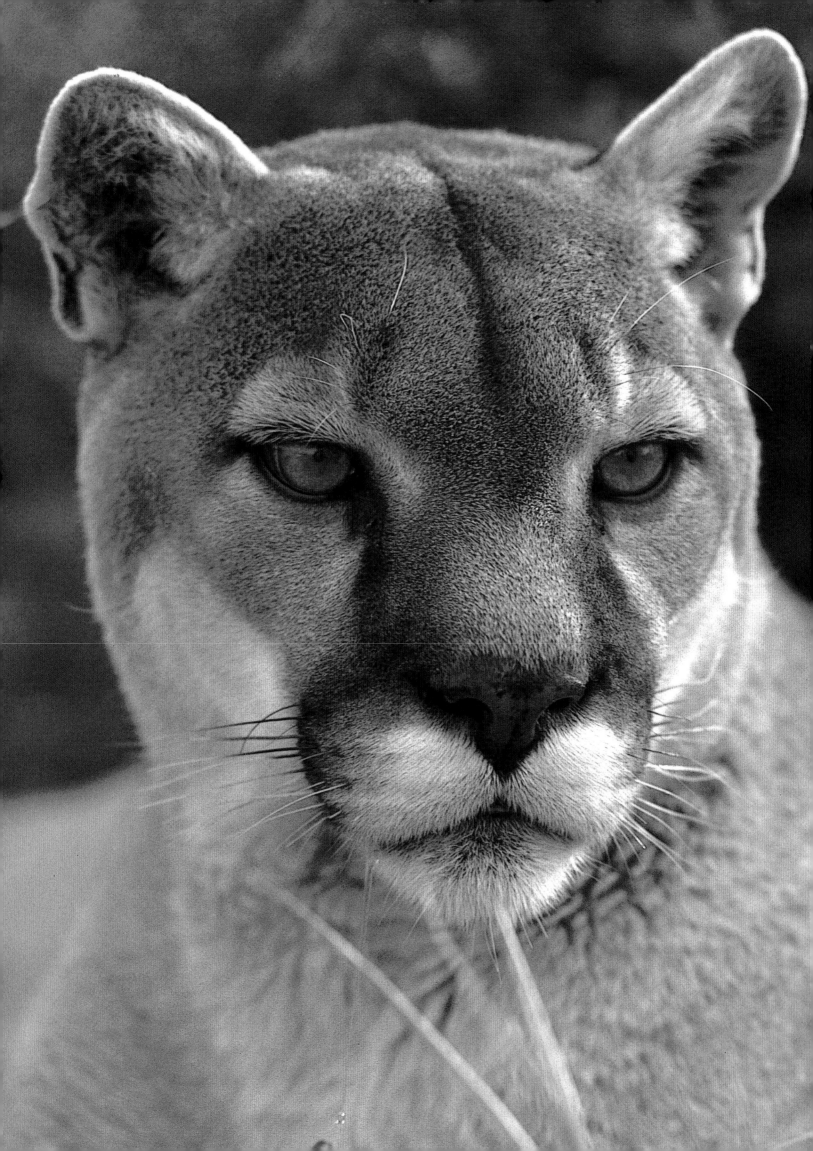

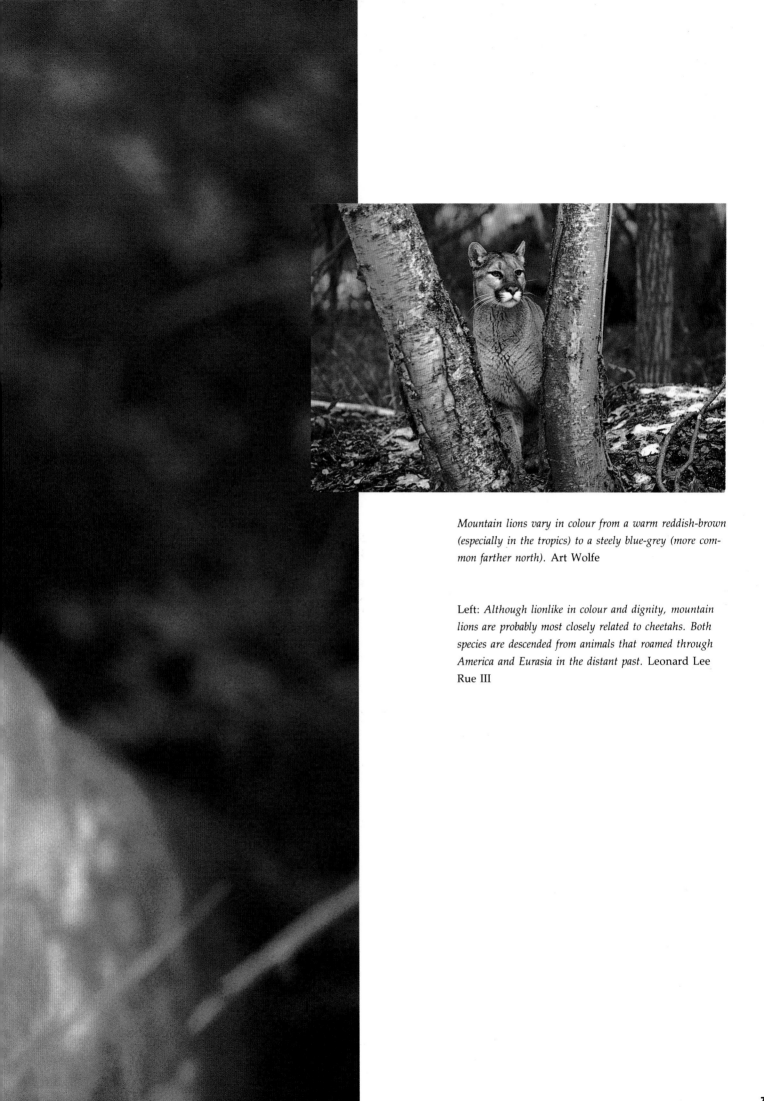

Mountain lions vary in colour from a warm reddish-brown (especially in the tropics) to a steely blue-grey (more common farther north). Art Wolfe

Left: *Although lionlike in colour and dignity, mountain lions are probably most closely related to cheetahs. Both species are descended from animals that roamed through America and Eurasia in the distant past.* Leonard Lee Rue III

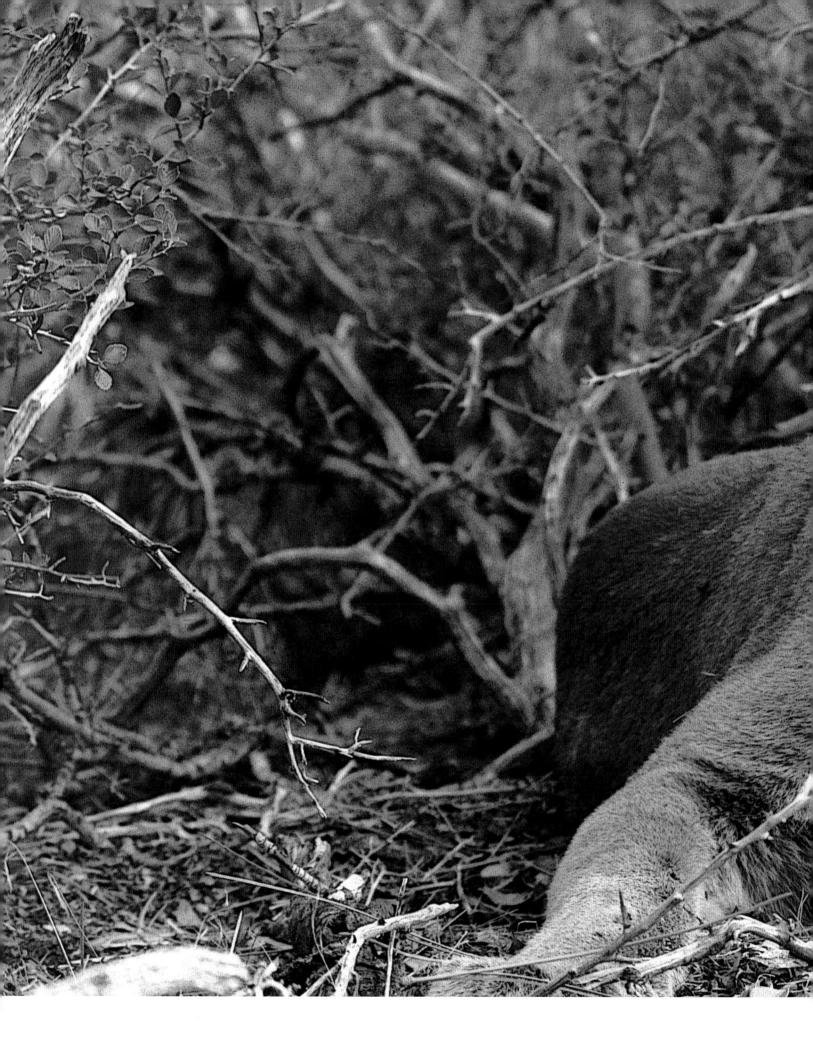

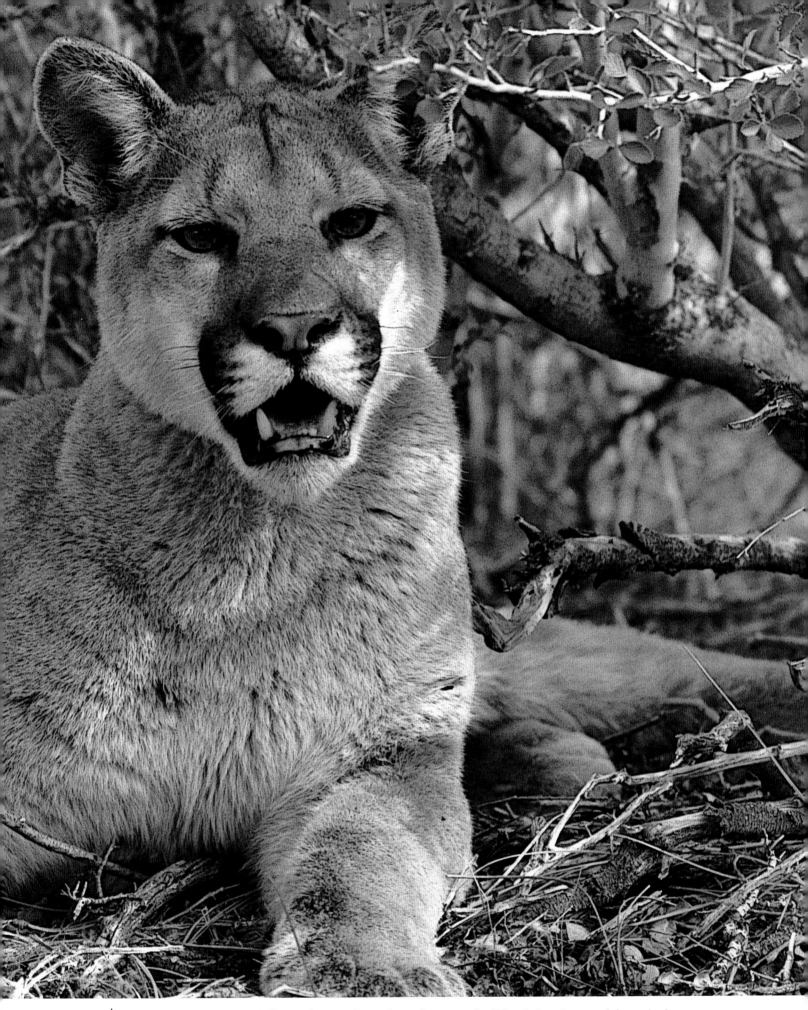

From the security of its day bed, a mountain lion snarls a warning against a close approach. Although the cats can and do survive in open country, they usually choose brushlands and forests that provide shelter for resting and cover for stalking prey. Leonard Lee Rue III

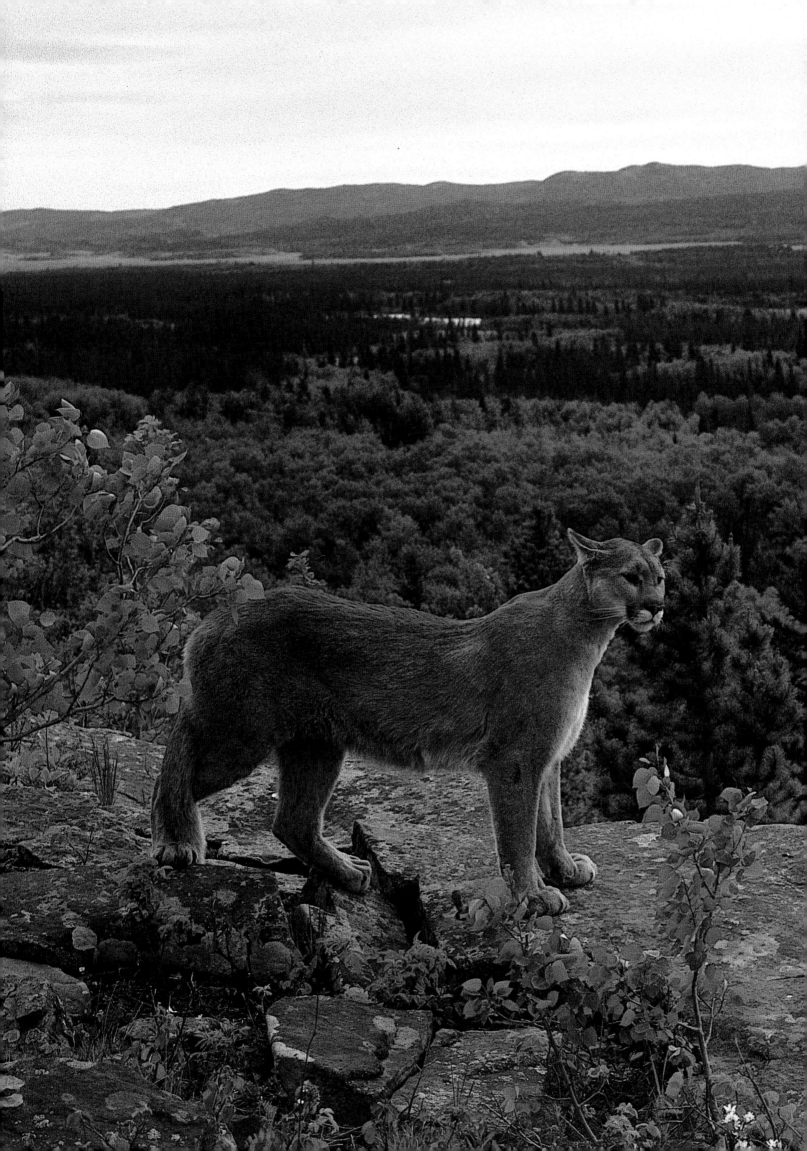

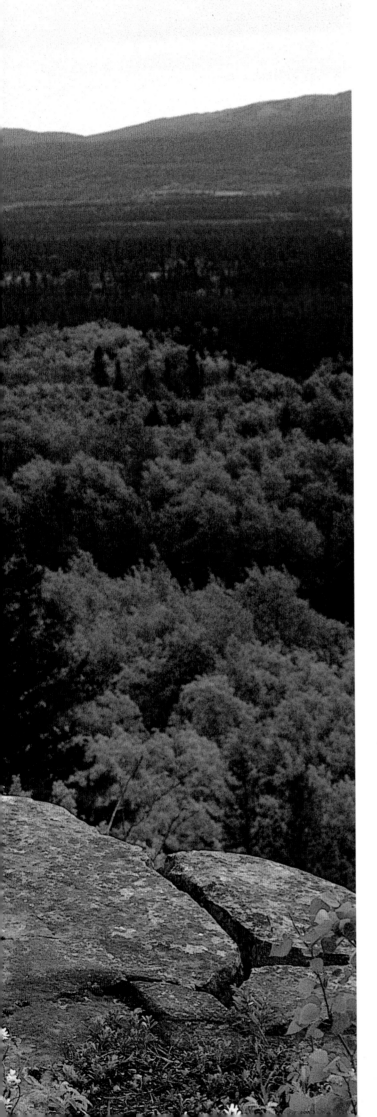

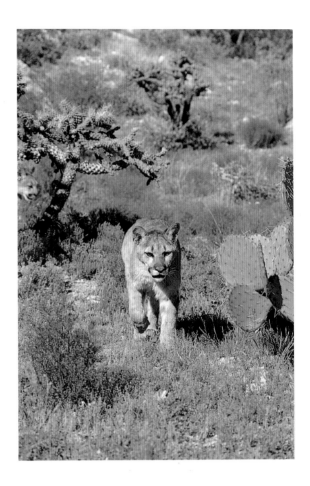

*A mountain lion strolls through the chaparral. The cats'
habitat includes canyon country, swamps, brushy stream-
sides, jungles and all manner of deciduous and coniferous
forests.* Stephen J. Krasemann/Valan Photos

Left: *Alert to signs or sounds of deer on the slopes below,
a mountain lion patrols the crest of a ridge in the Rocky
Mountain foothills. Now plentiful only in the west, mountain lions were common across North America before
European settlement.* Halle Flygare/Valan Photos

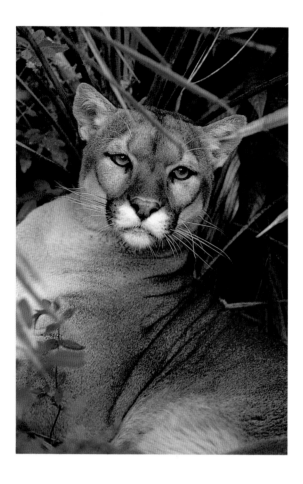

Florida panthers, the only population of mountain lions known to survive in eastern North America, are themselves severely endangered. With an average of one thousand people moving into the state each day, the cats' living space is being lost to housing and orange groves. Steve Kaufman

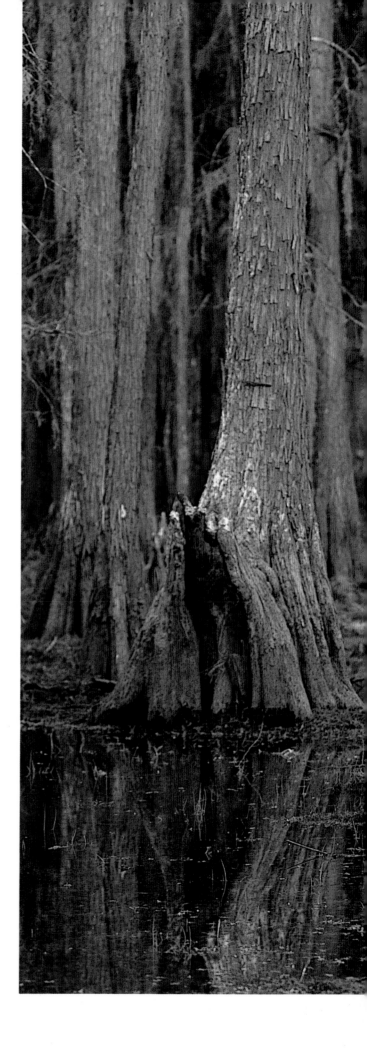

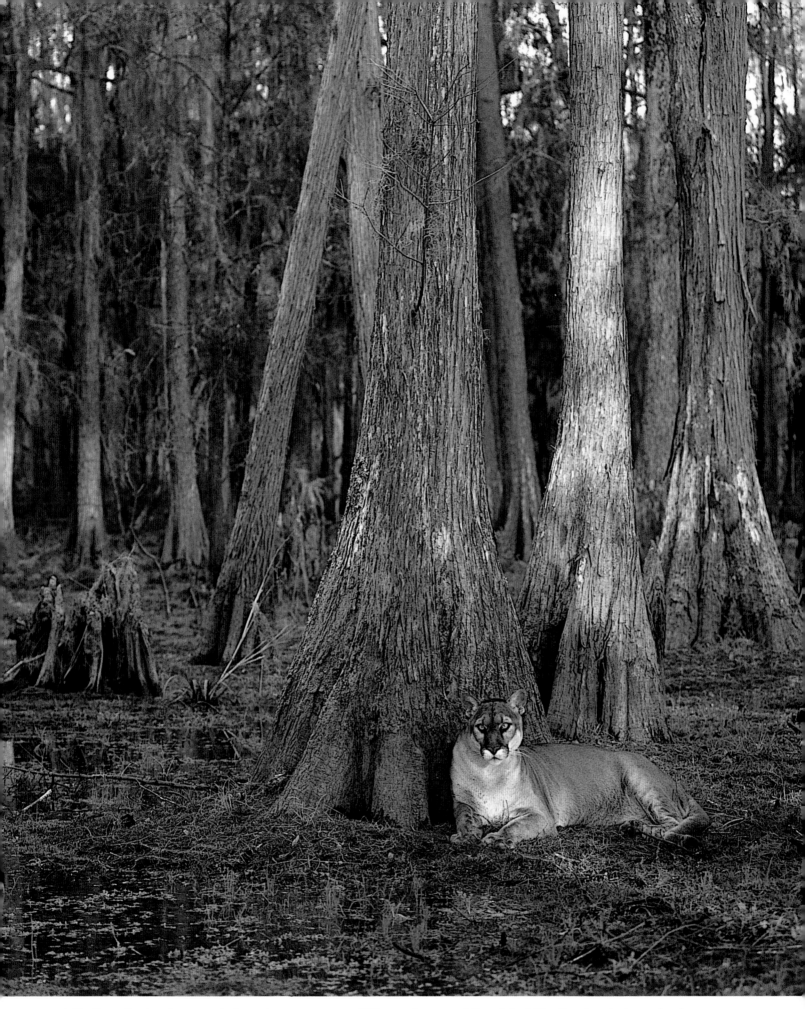

A Florida panther lounges on a mat of moss in a cypress swamp. With a maximum population of about fifty, the subspecies is now largely restricted to the Big Cypress and Everglades districts. Tom & Pat Leeson

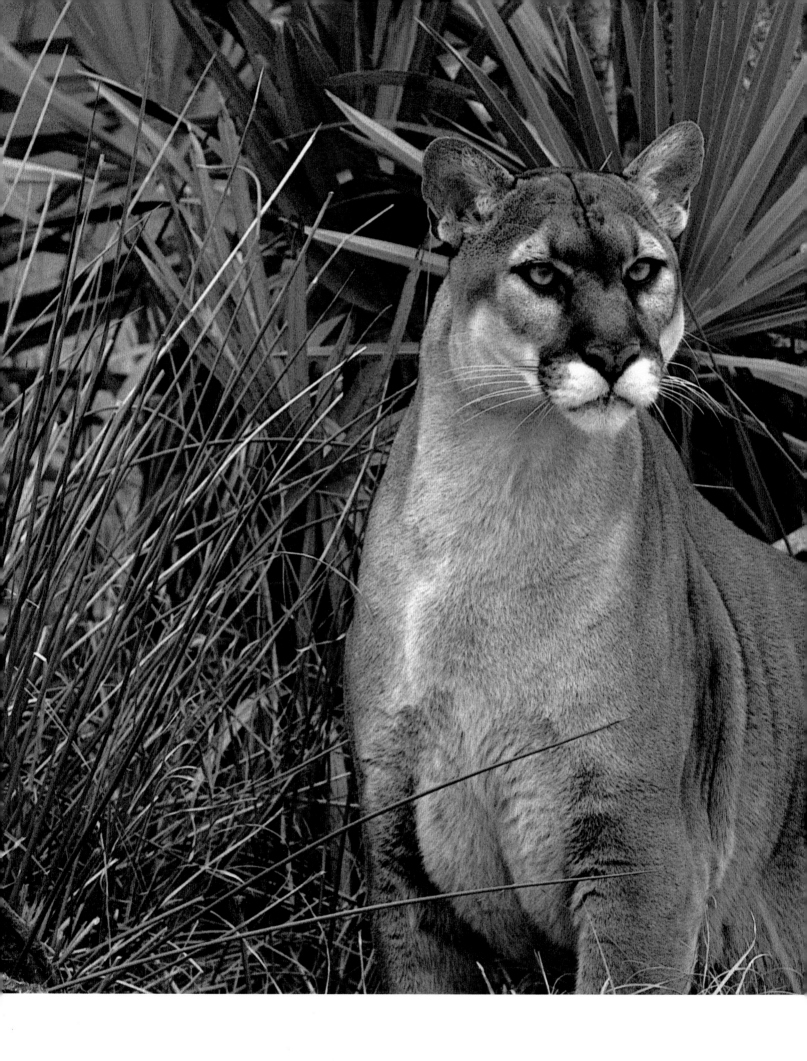

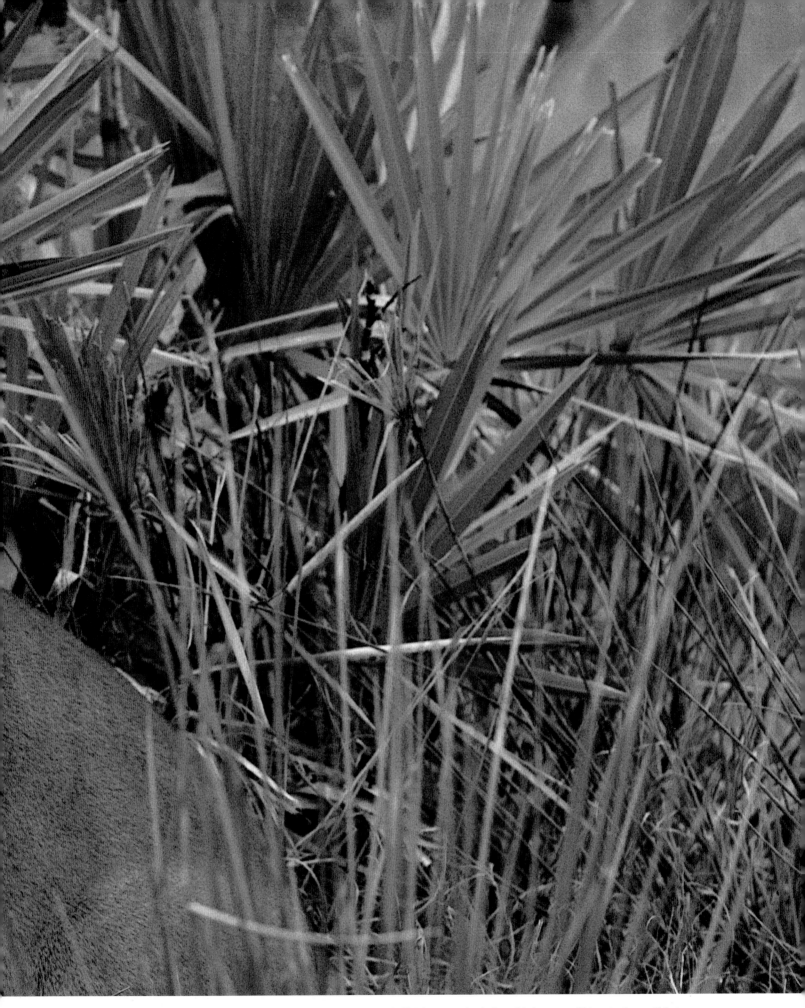

The natural majesty of the Florida panther has won it the designation of official state animal. But this honour will lose its lustre if last-minute efforts to rescue the panther prove futile. Tom & Pat Leeson

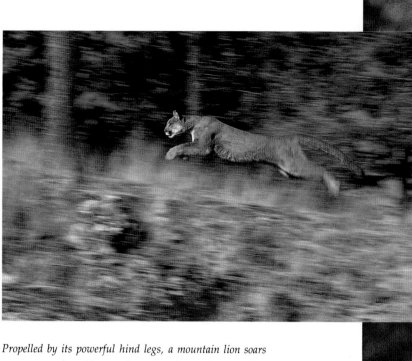

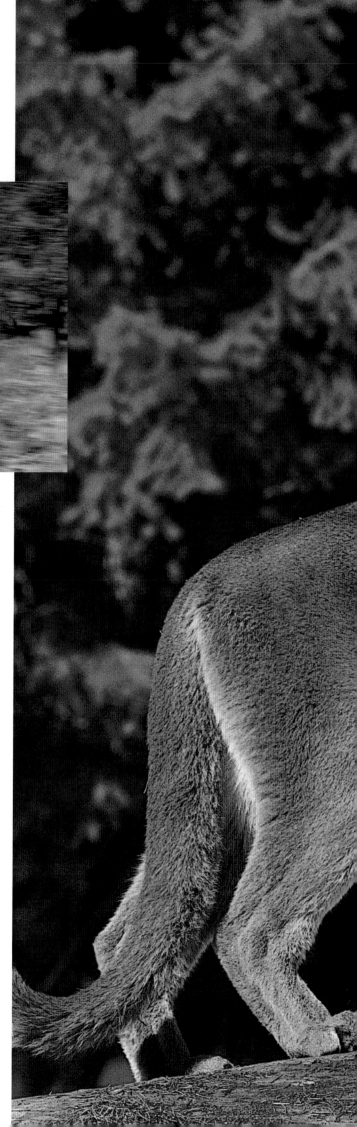

Propelled by its powerful hind legs, a mountain lion soars across a meadow. The cats have been known to cover 13 metres (45 feet) in a single, arching bound—about the width of a city lot. Ascending a cliff, they can leap 5.5 metres (18 feet), or about two storeys up. Erwin & Peggy Bauer

Right: *With its muscled shoulders and barrel chest, this mountain lion creates the impression that it can take care of itself. But physical strength is no protection against the force of industrial society. Of the animals that have vanished from the Earth in the past four centuries, half have been "high-and-mighty" predators.* Tom Walker

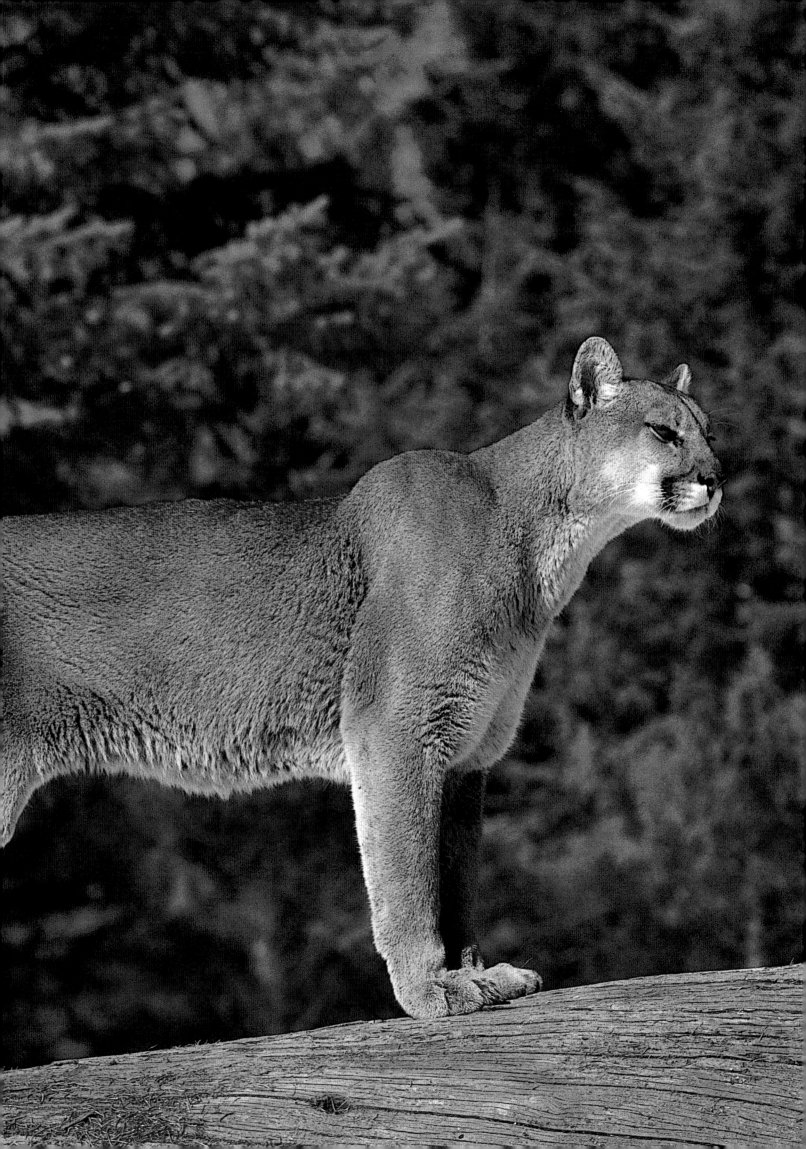

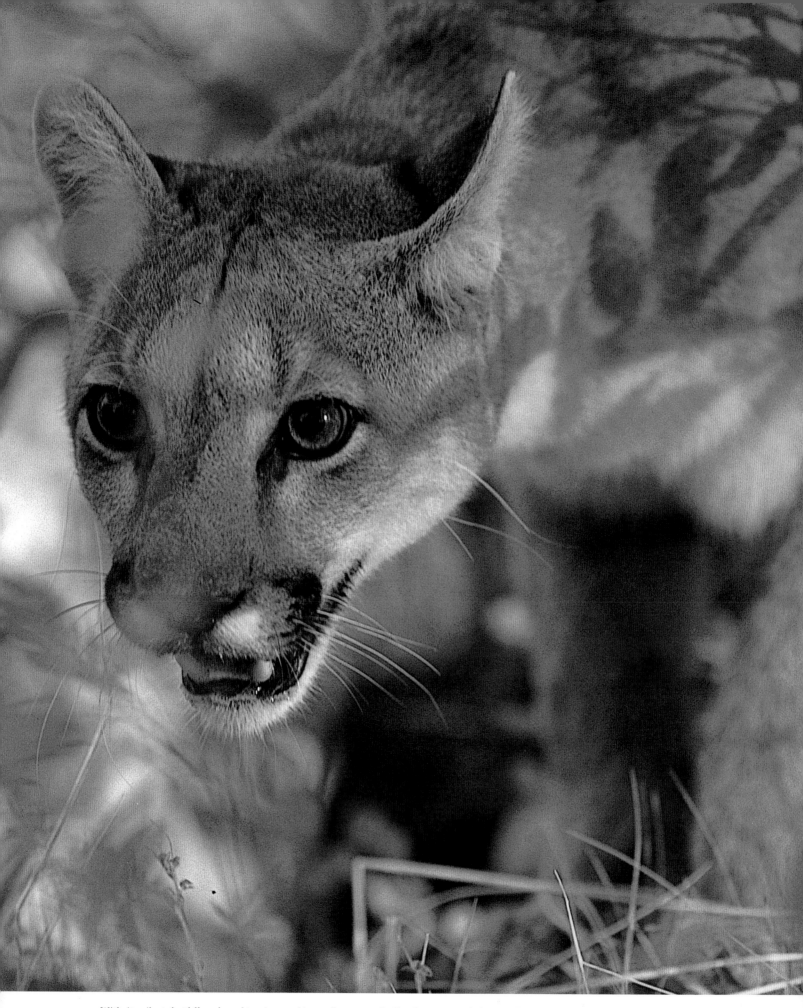

With its silent footfall and unobtrusive markings, the mountain lion has mastered the art of invisibility. Because it is not built for long-distance running, the lion sneaks up on its prey and springs at it from close range. Denver Bryan

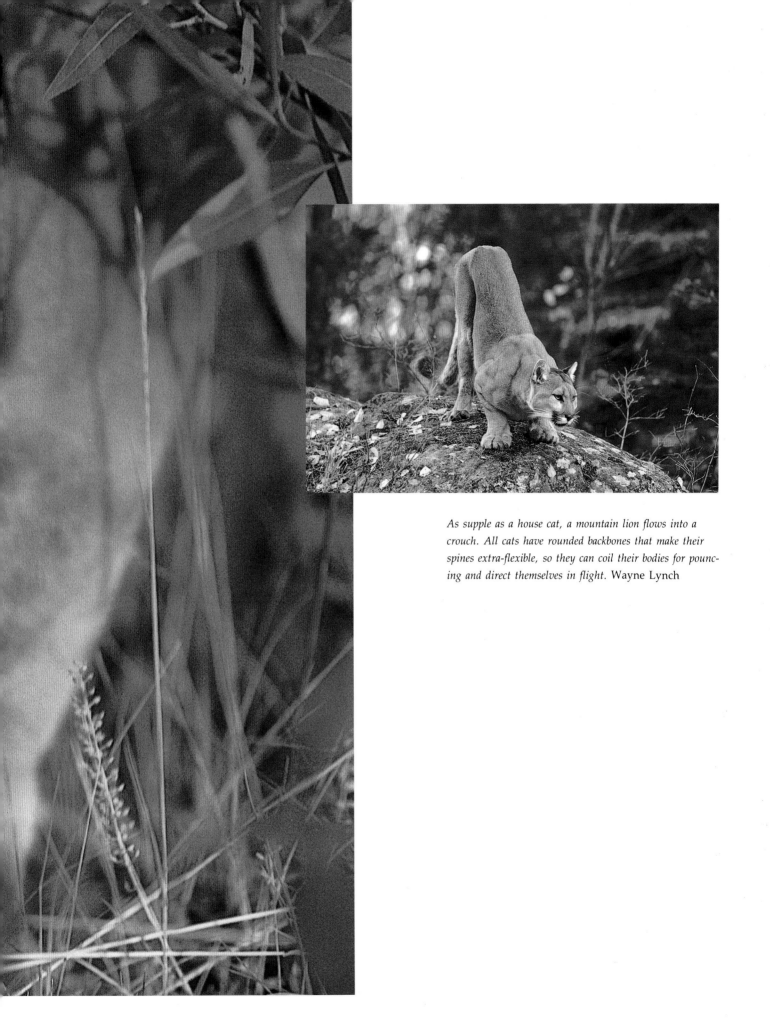

As supple as a house cat, a mountain lion flows into a crouch. All cats have rounded backbones that make their spines extra-flexible, so they can coil their bodies for pouncing and direct themselves in flight. Wayne Lynch

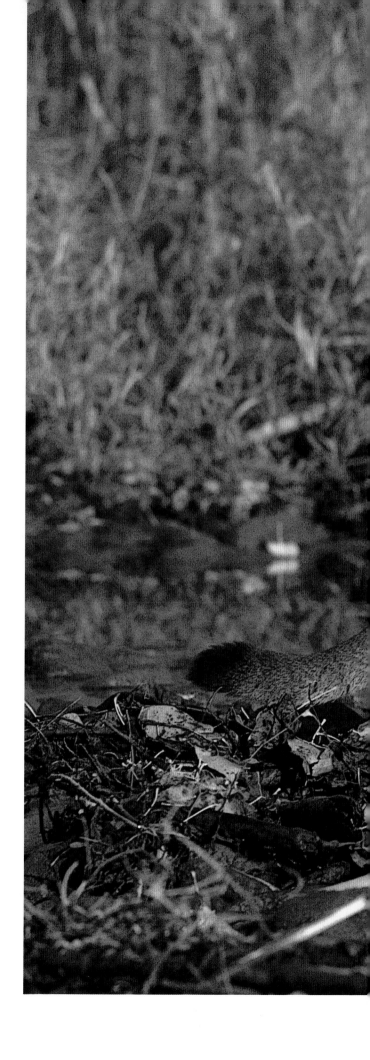

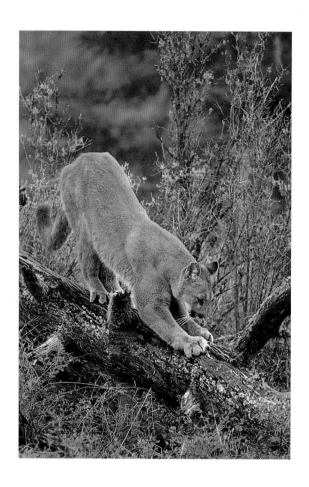

With its tail poised for balance, a mountain lion hones its claws. When not in use, the claws are sheathed inside the paws so they stay piercingly sharp. Thomas Kitchin

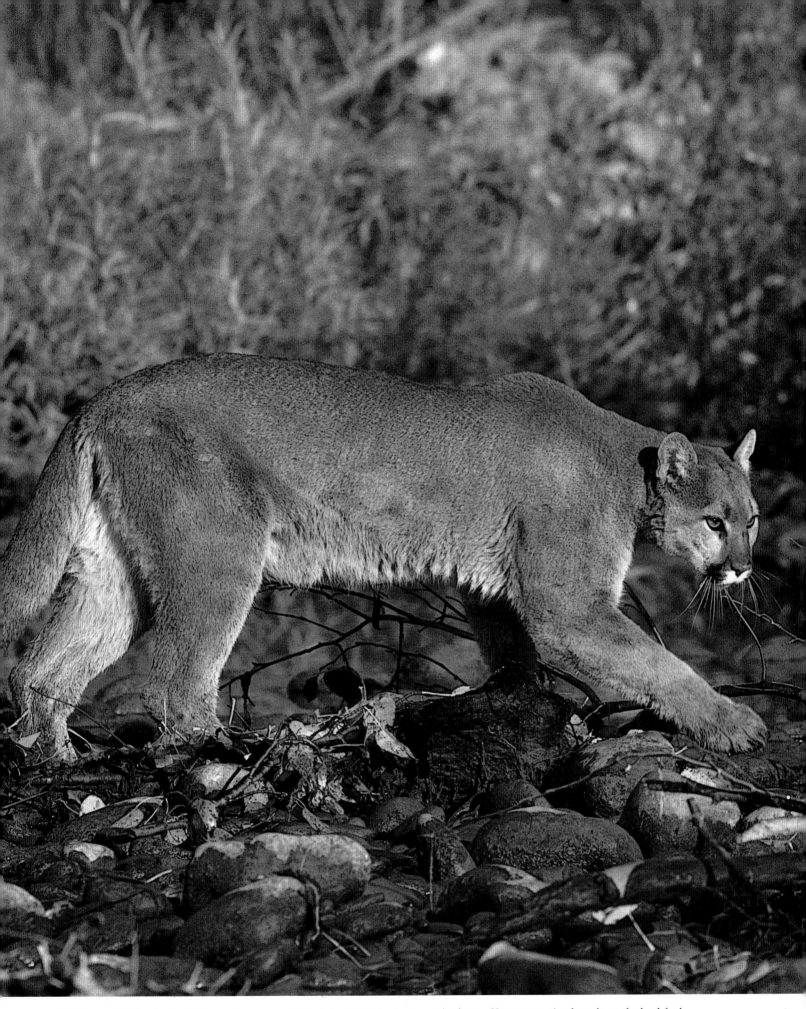

Each mountain lion hunts in its own home area, which it travels tirelessly in search of prey. Home-range size depends on the local food supply, but as a rule, a cat needs 50 to 300 square kilometres of living space (20 to 115 square miles). Alan & Sandy Carey

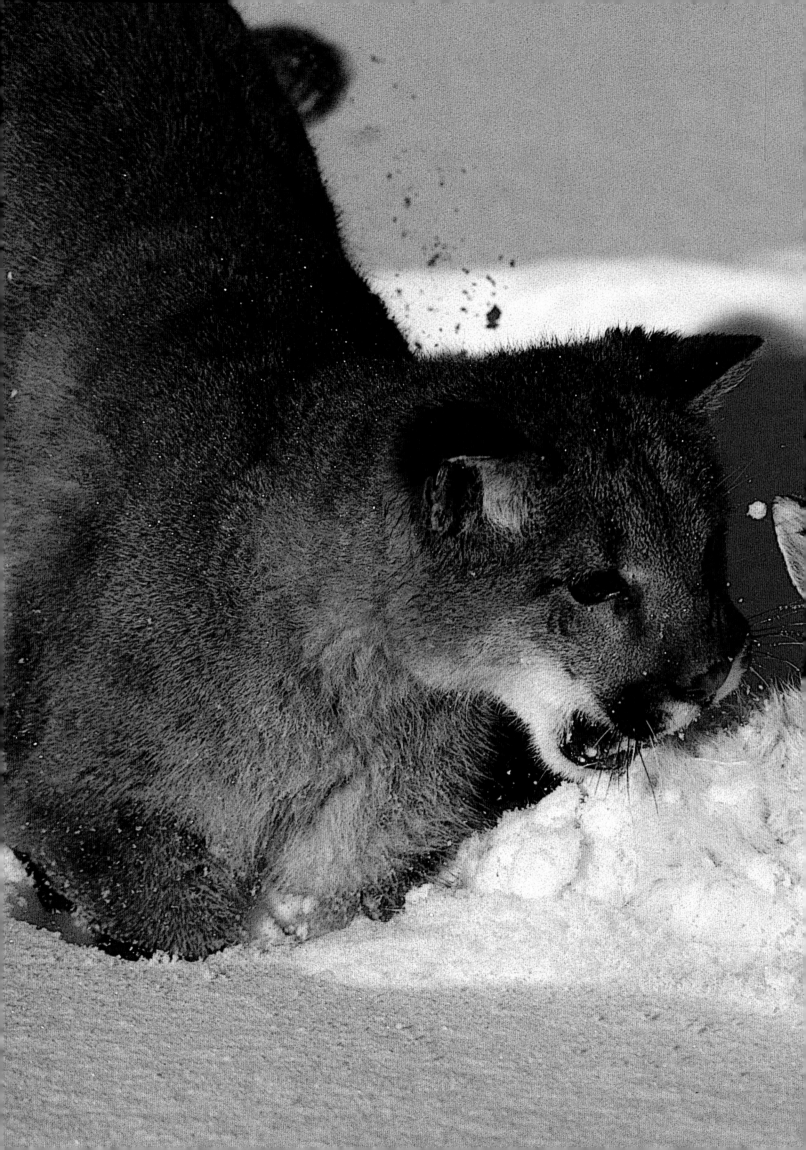

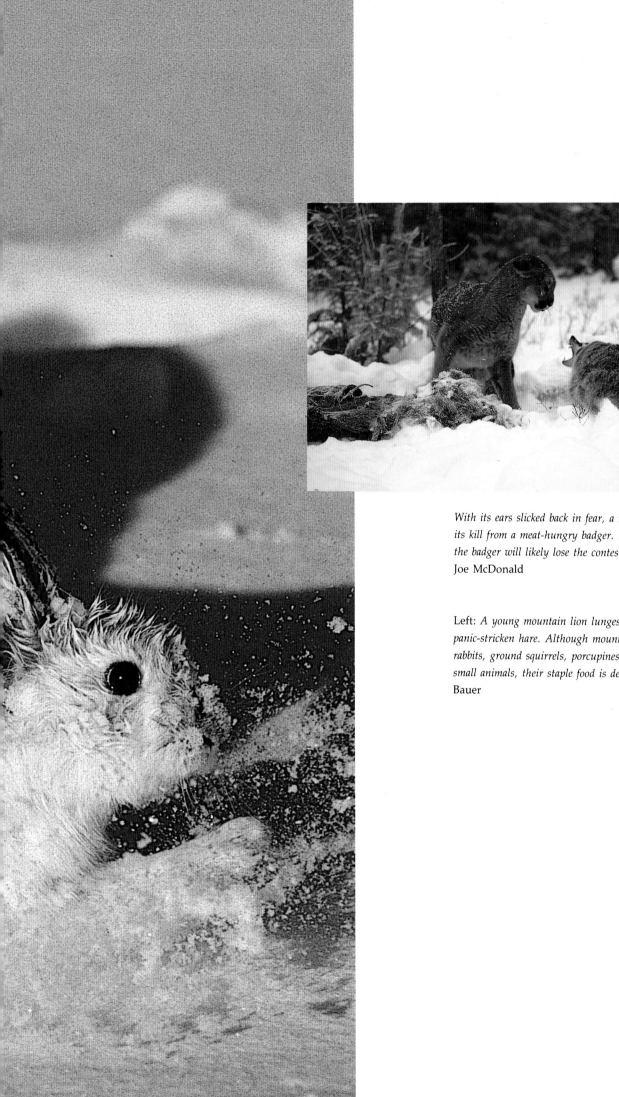

With its ears slicked back in fear, a mountain lion defends its kill from a meat-hungry badger. For all of its ferocity, the badger will likely lose the contest and, perhaps, its life. Joe McDonald

Left: *A young mountain lion lunges towards the neck of a panic-stricken hare. Although mountain lions eat hares, rabbits, ground squirrels, porcupines, bobcats and other small animals, their staple food is deer.* Erwin & Peggy Bauer

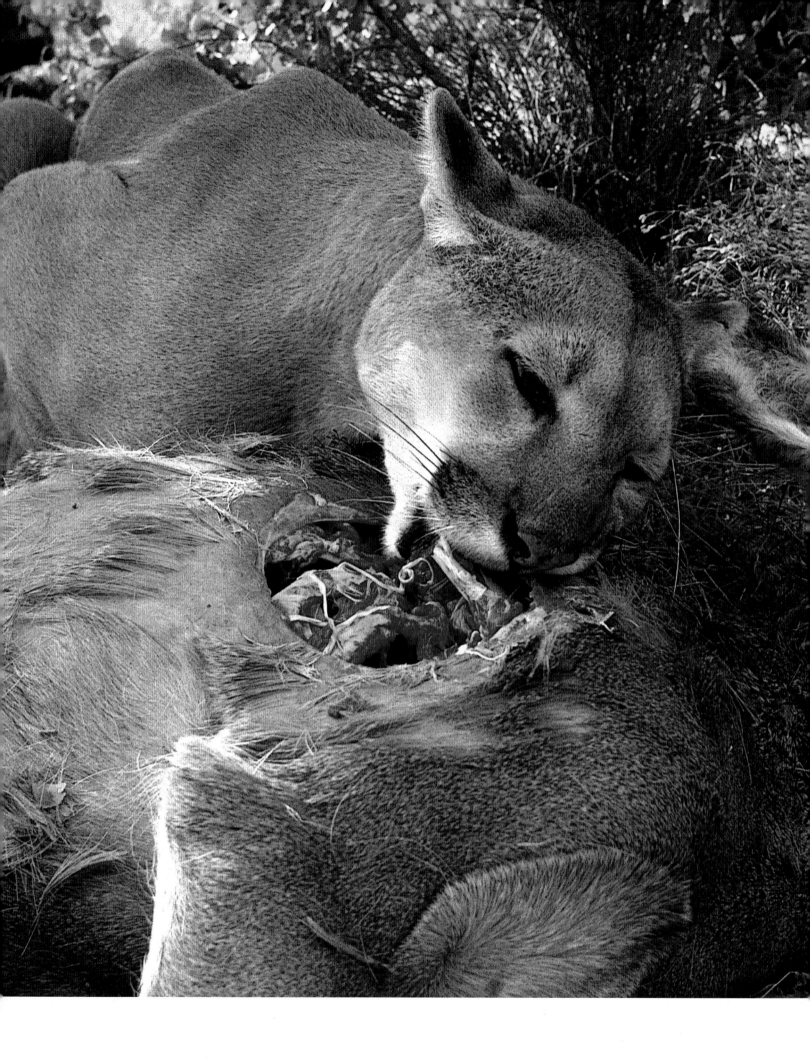

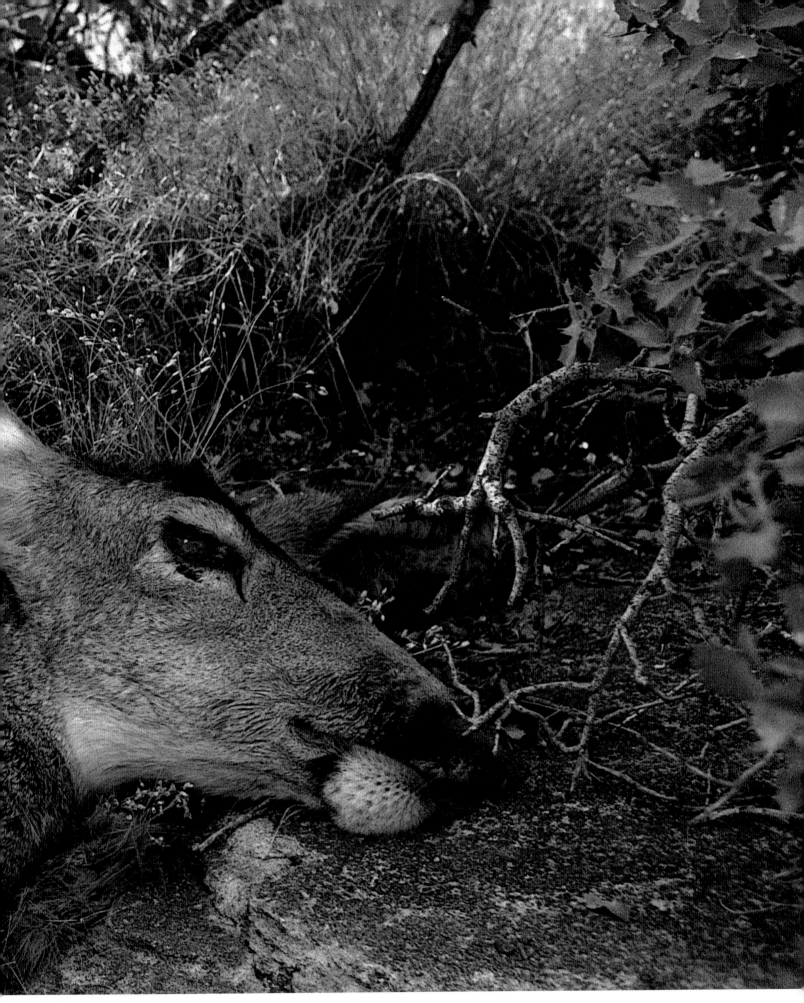

Like house cats, mountain lions often pluck the hair off their prey before eating it. Here, a mountain lion feeds on a freshly killed mule deer. When it has had enough, the cat will partially cover the carcass with soil and leaves and return to it several times in the next two or three weeks. Stephen J. Krasemann/Valan Photos

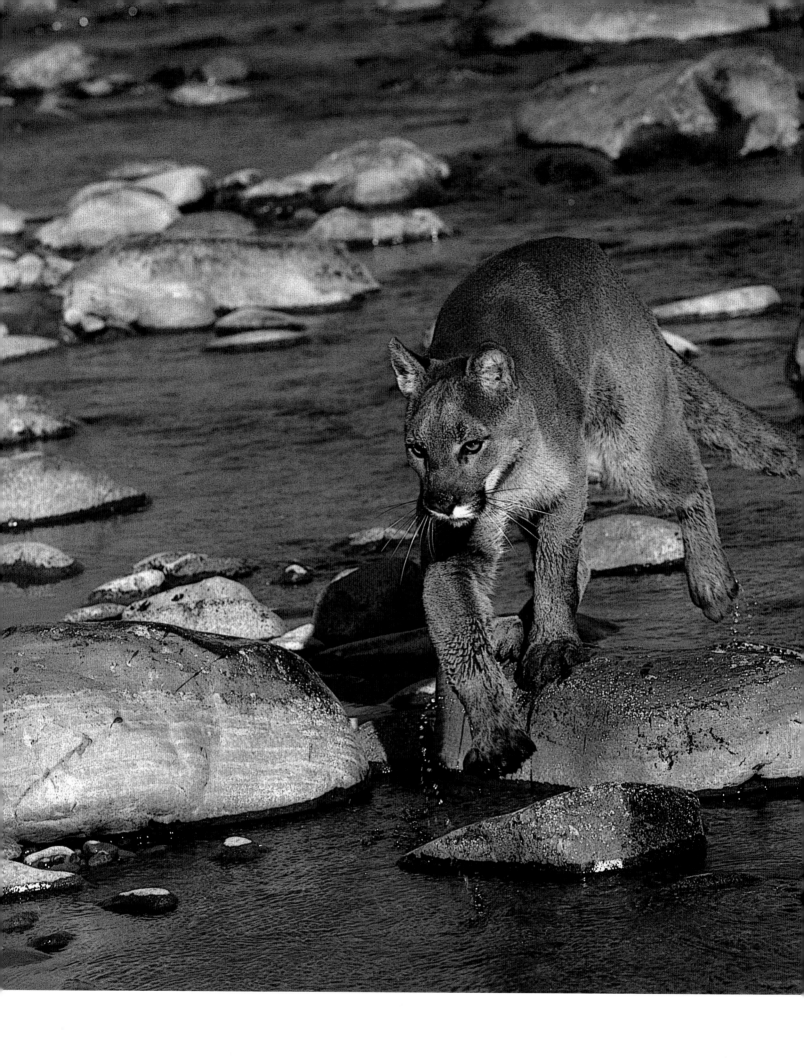

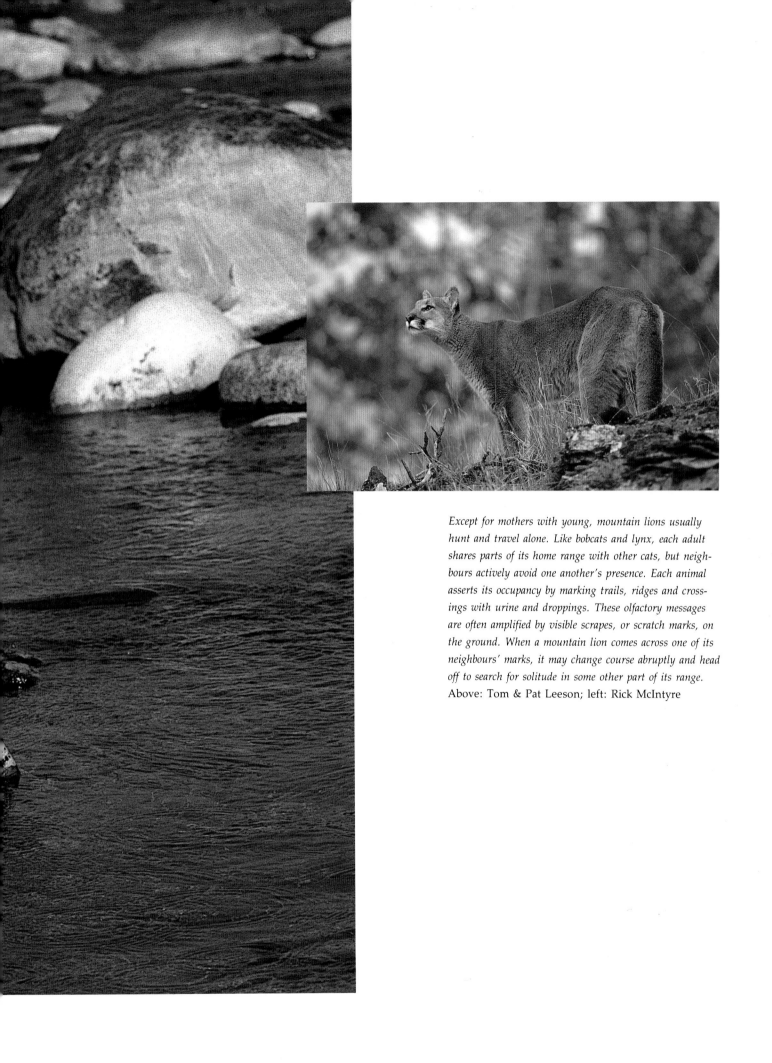

Except for mothers with young, mountain lions usually hunt and travel alone. Like bobcats and lynx, each adult shares parts of its home range with other cats, but neighbours actively avoid one another's presence. Each animal asserts its occupancy by marking trails, ridges and crossings with urine and droppings. These olfactory messages are often amplified by visible scrapes, or scratch marks, on the ground. When a mountain lion comes across one of its neighbours' marks, it may change course abruptly and head off to search for solitude in some other part of its range.
Above: Tom & Pat Leeson; left: Rick McIntyre

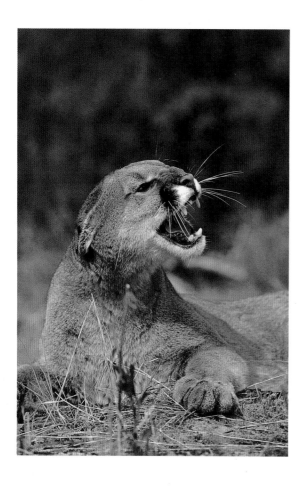

Although mountain lions cannot roar, they certainly can yowl. When a female is ready to breed, she announces her condition with raucous squalls. Tom & Pat Leeson

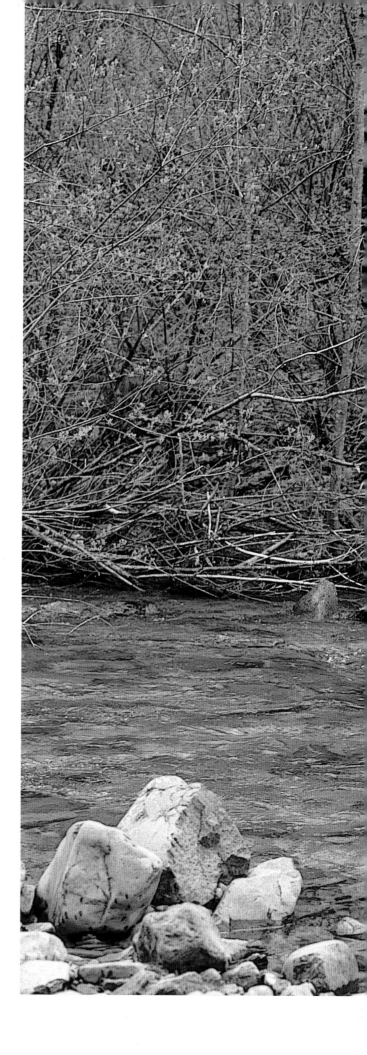

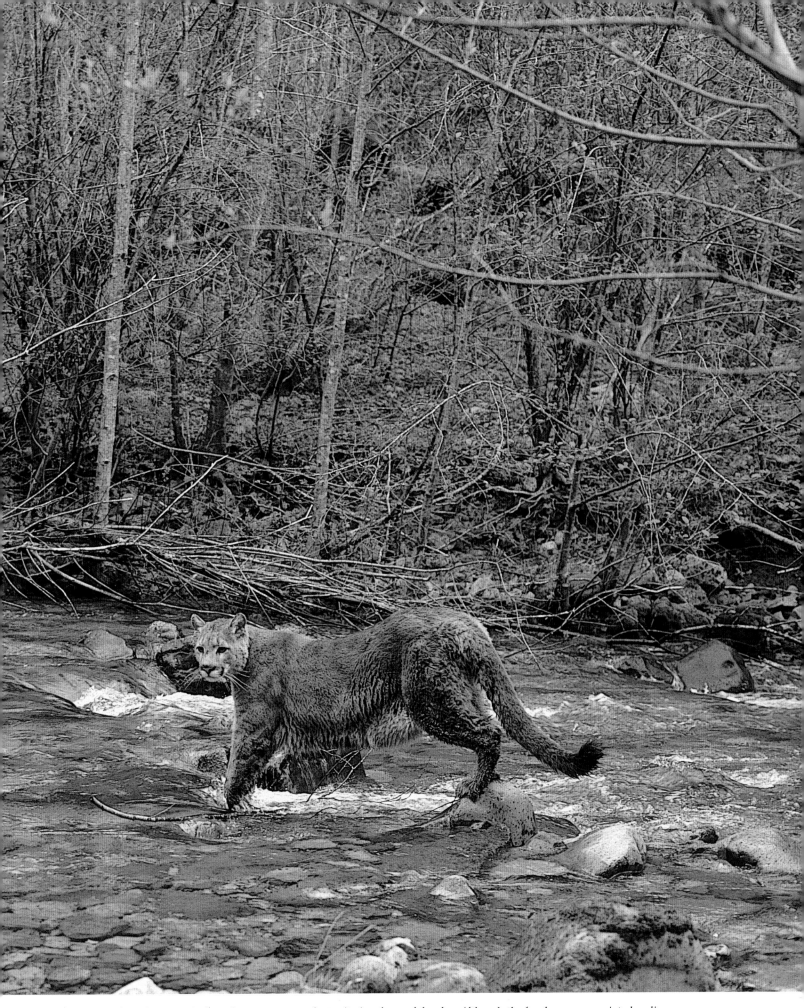

The range of a male mountain lion often encompasses the territories of several females. Although the females may come into breeding condition at any time of the year, the potential mates somehow manage to find each other, undeterred by weather, terrain or long distances.
Tom & Pat Leeson

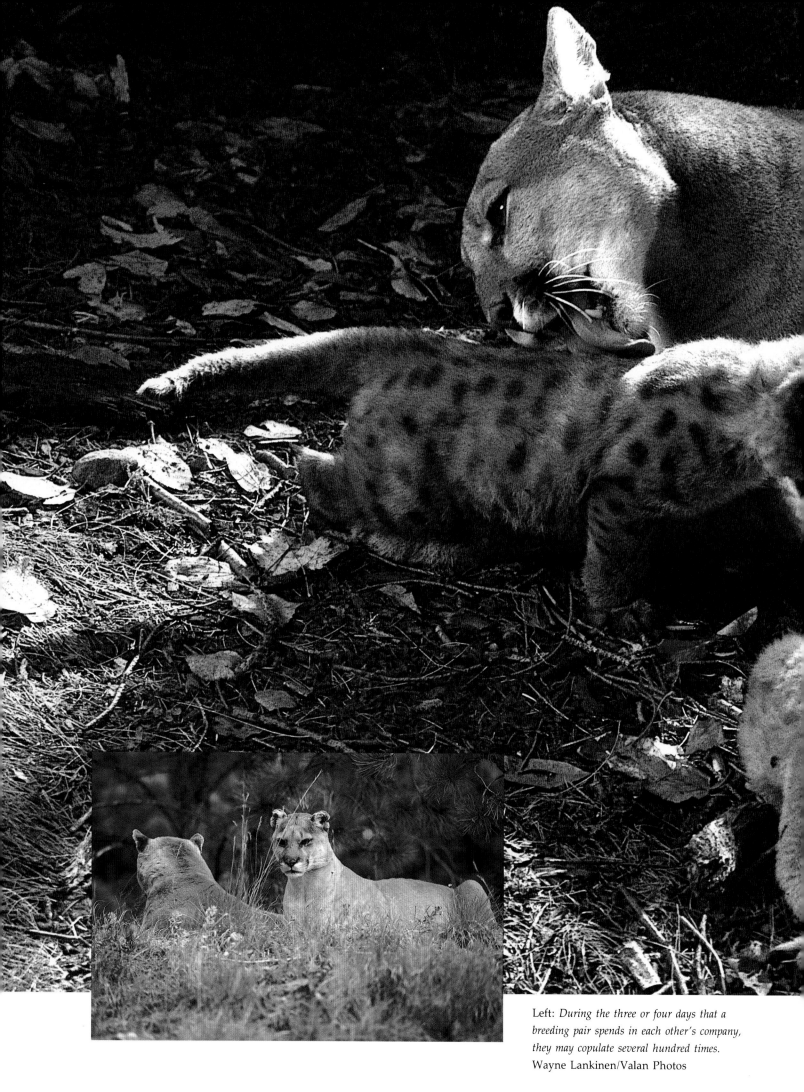

Left: *During the three or four days that a breeding pair spends in each other's company, they may copulate several hundred times.*
Wayne Lankinen/Valan Photos

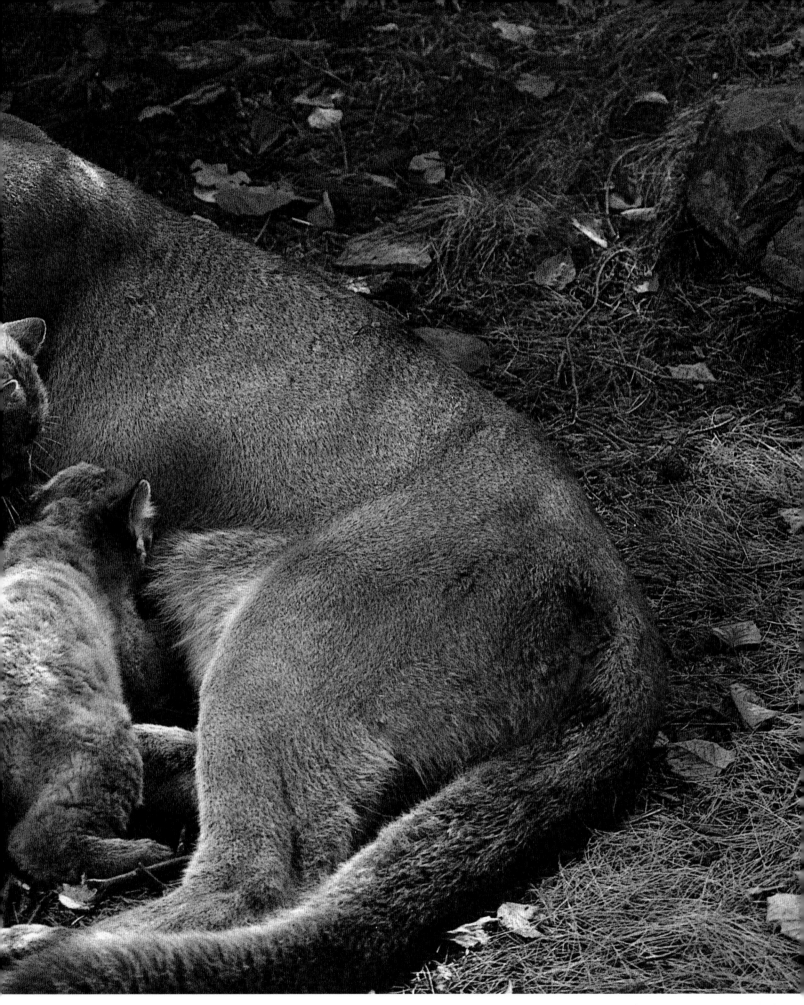

A female mountain lion cleans and nurses her dappled kittens. Although litters of up to six kittens have been recorded, twins and triplets are most common. They will nurse for about two months. Erwin & Peggy Bauer

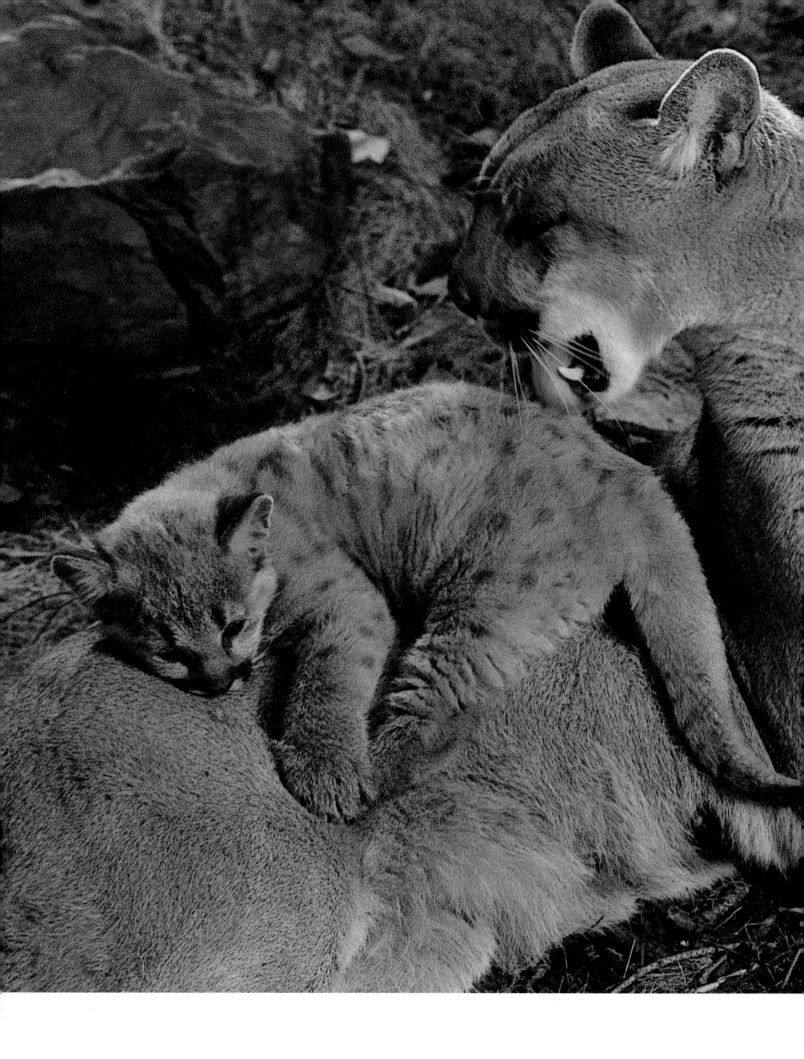

A young kitten makes the most of its mother's company. Mountain lions bear their young in rock slides, crevices and caves, under uprooted trees and in dense thickets. Erwin & Peggy Bauer

102

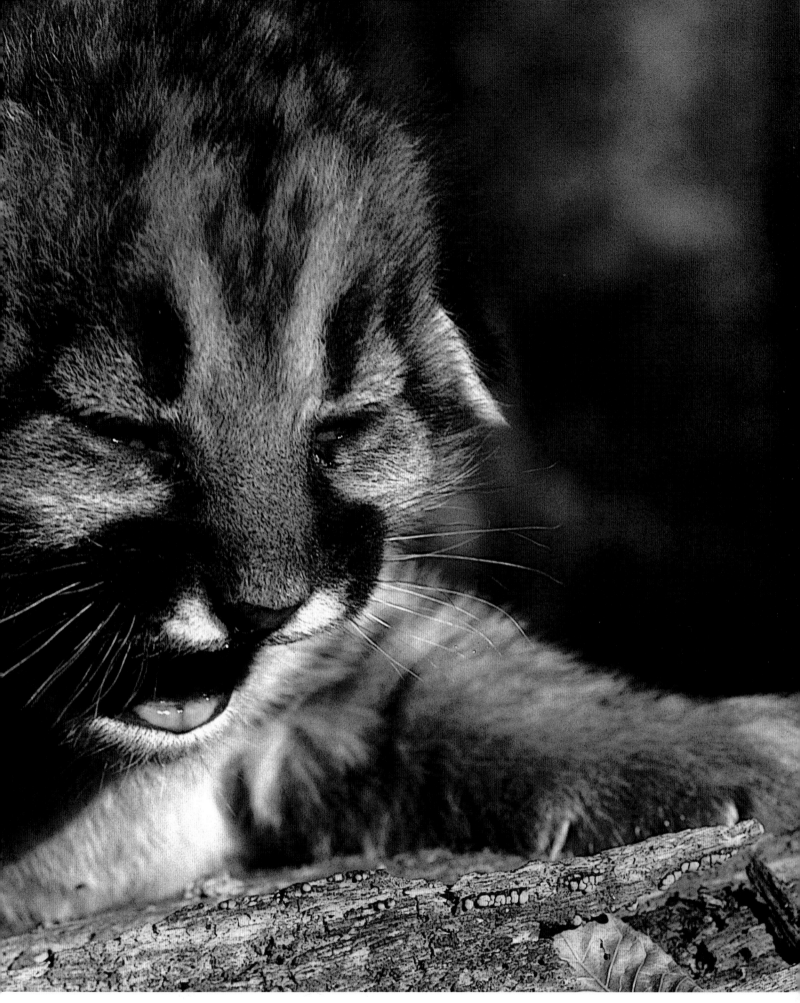

The mighty mountain lion at age two weeks. Its baby-blue eyes will begin to turn dark at about eight months. Leonard Lee Rue III

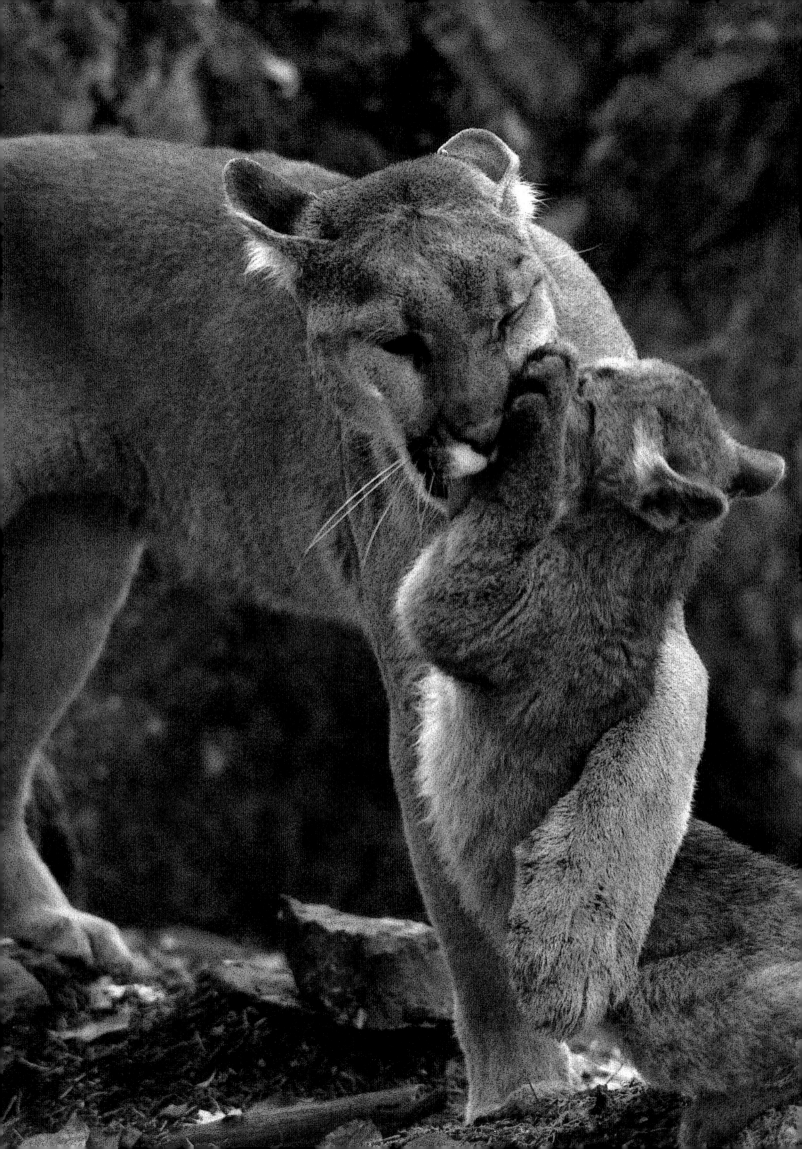

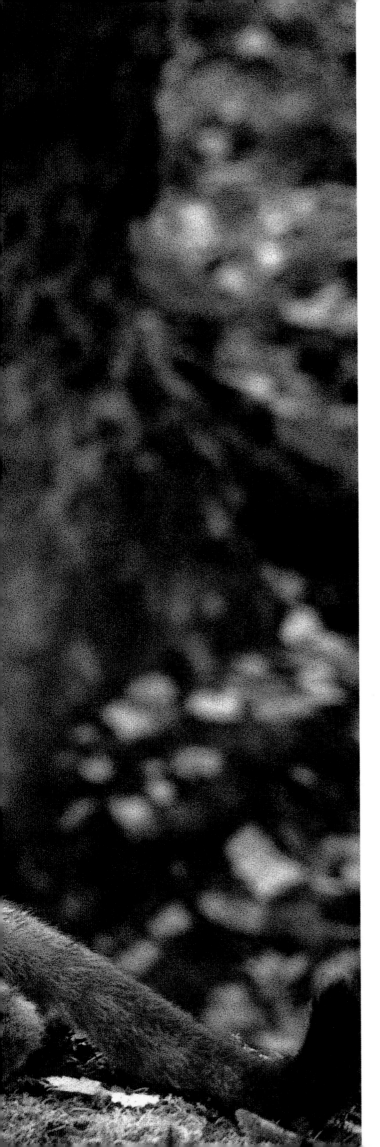

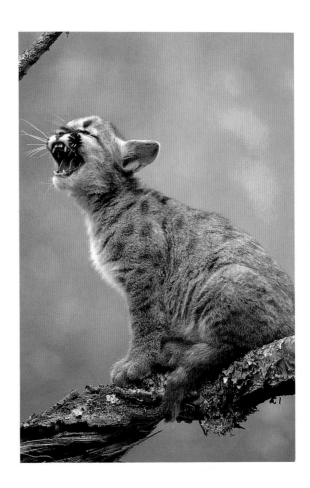

Mountain lions meow, scream, growl, purr, spit and hiss, just like domestic cats, only much louder. Kittens also have a vocabulary of birdlike whistles and chirps. Wayne Lynch

Left: *A female mountain lion nuzzles her kitten. The mother stays with her kittens constantly in the beginning, but later she leaves them in hiding for days while she is off hunting.* Erwin & Peggy Bauer

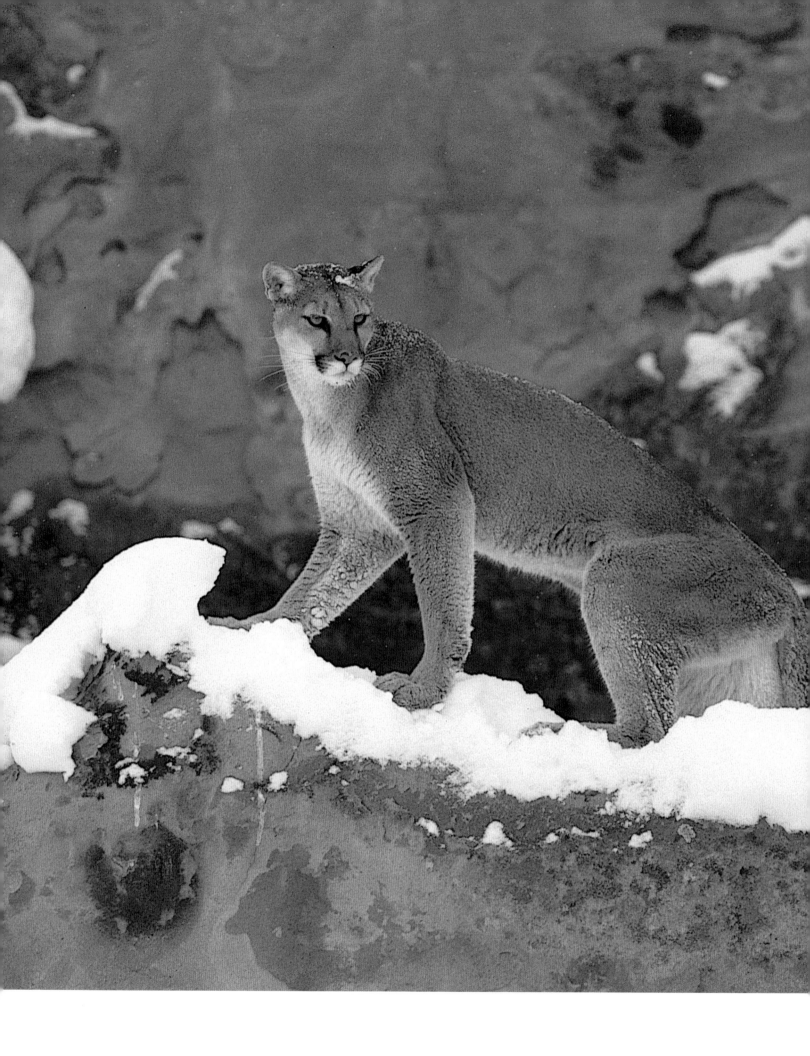

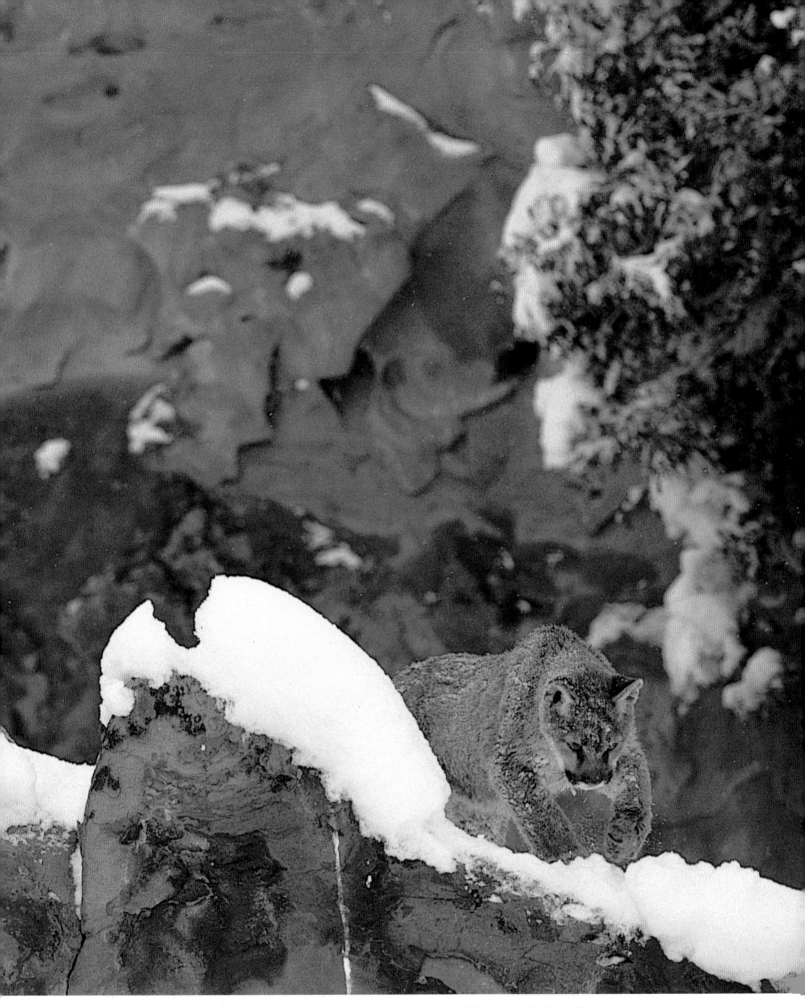

A female mountain lion and her kitten walk along a natural catwalk in the Colorado Rockies, U.S.A. W. Perry Conway

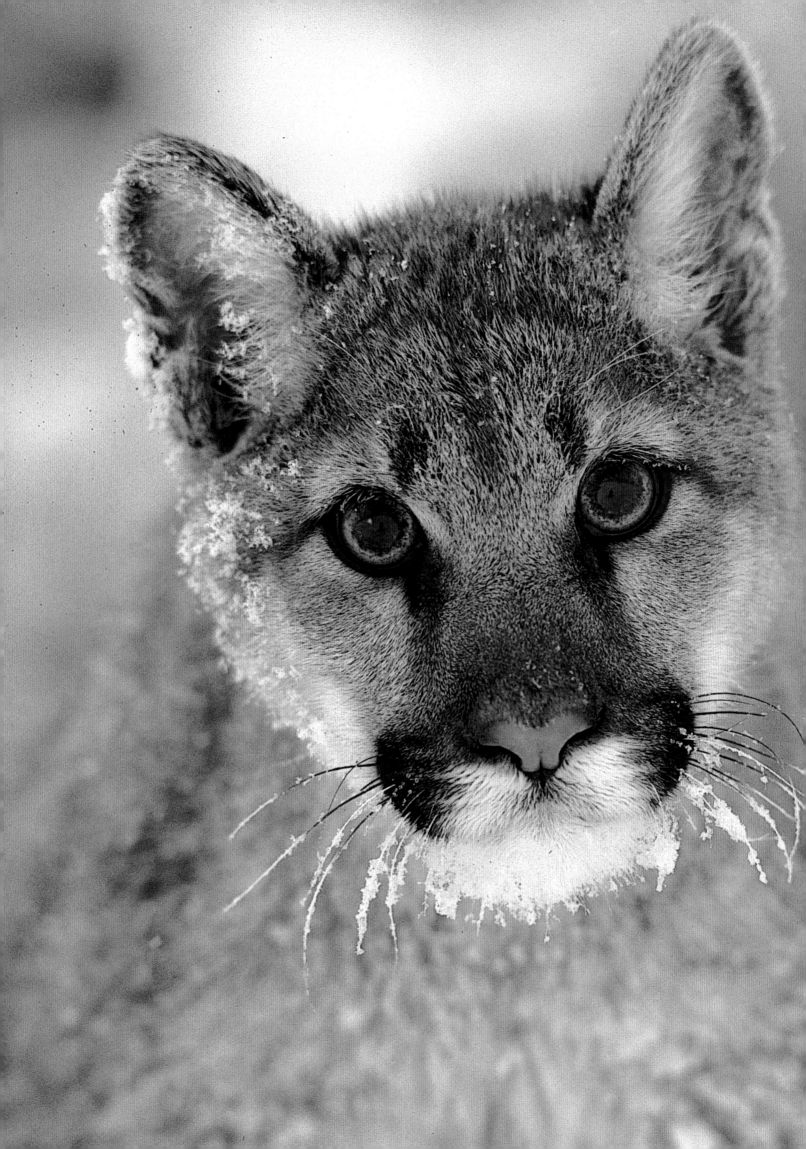

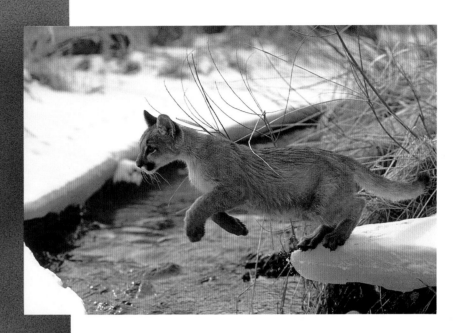

When mountain lion kittens are very young, the mother carries meat to them at the den. Later, when they are able to travel through rugged country, she will lead them to her kills. Denver Bryan

Left: *Although clearly recognizable as a mountain lion, this youngster still wears traces of its infant spots.* W. Perry Conway

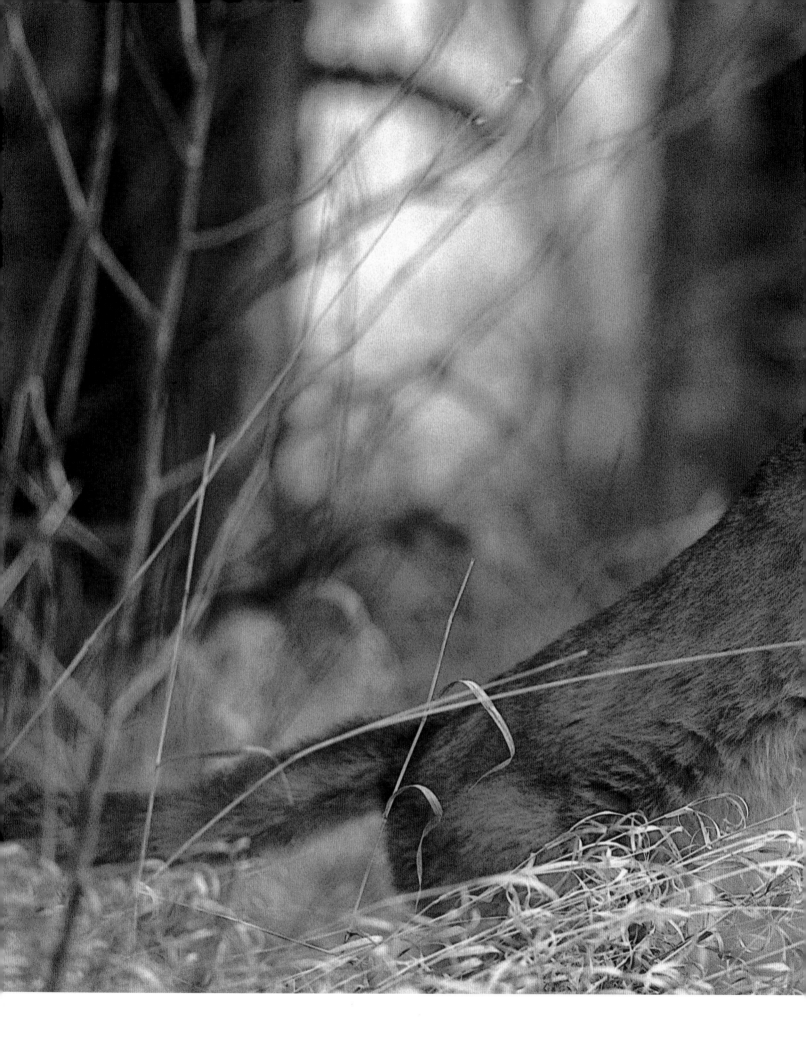

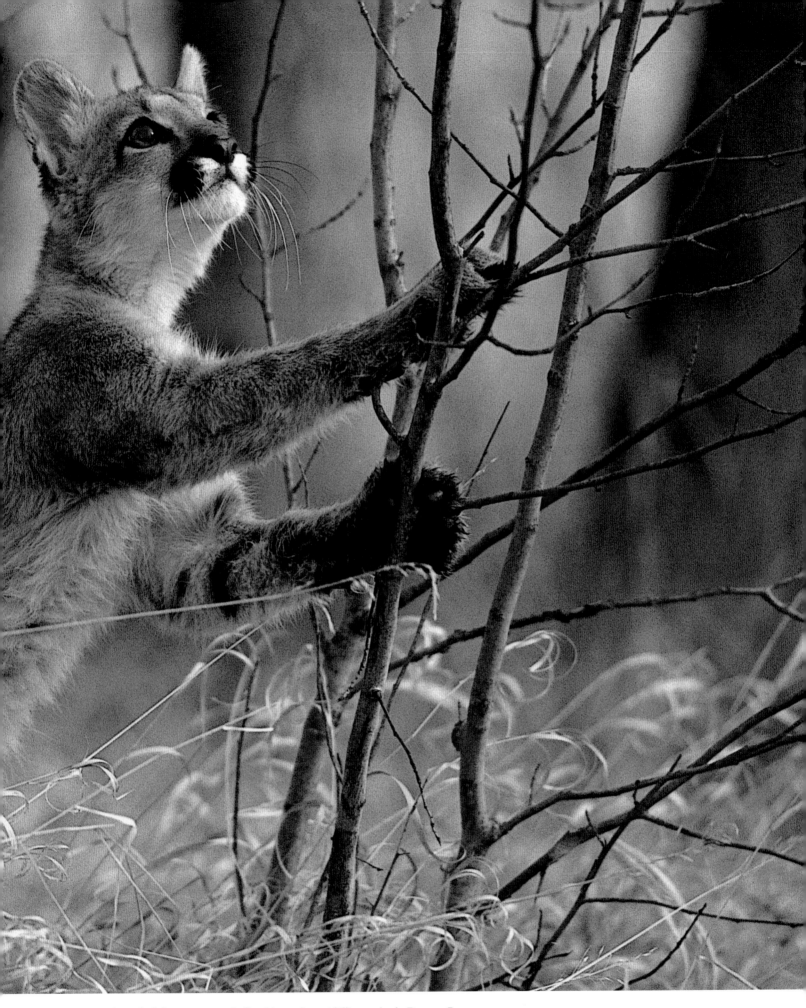

Intent on its make-believe, a mountain lion kitten plays at killing a shrub. Denver Bryan

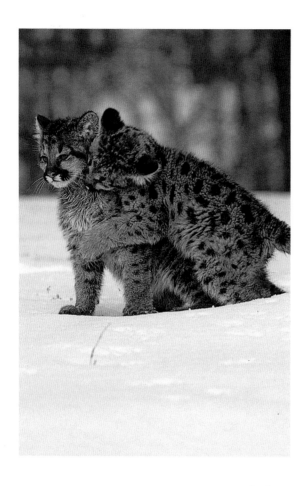

Mountain lion kittens are frisky and busy, with a lively, "into-everything" curiosity. Through play, they practise behaviours they will later employ in hunting and social or sexual encounters. Above and right: Alan & Sandy Carey

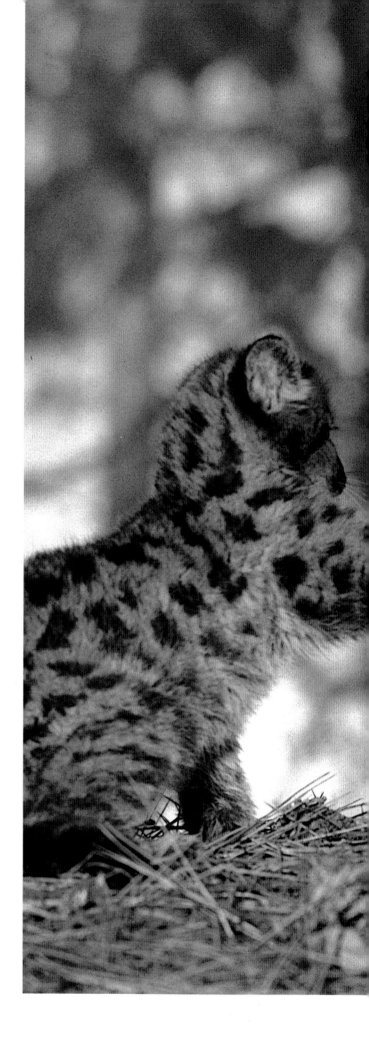

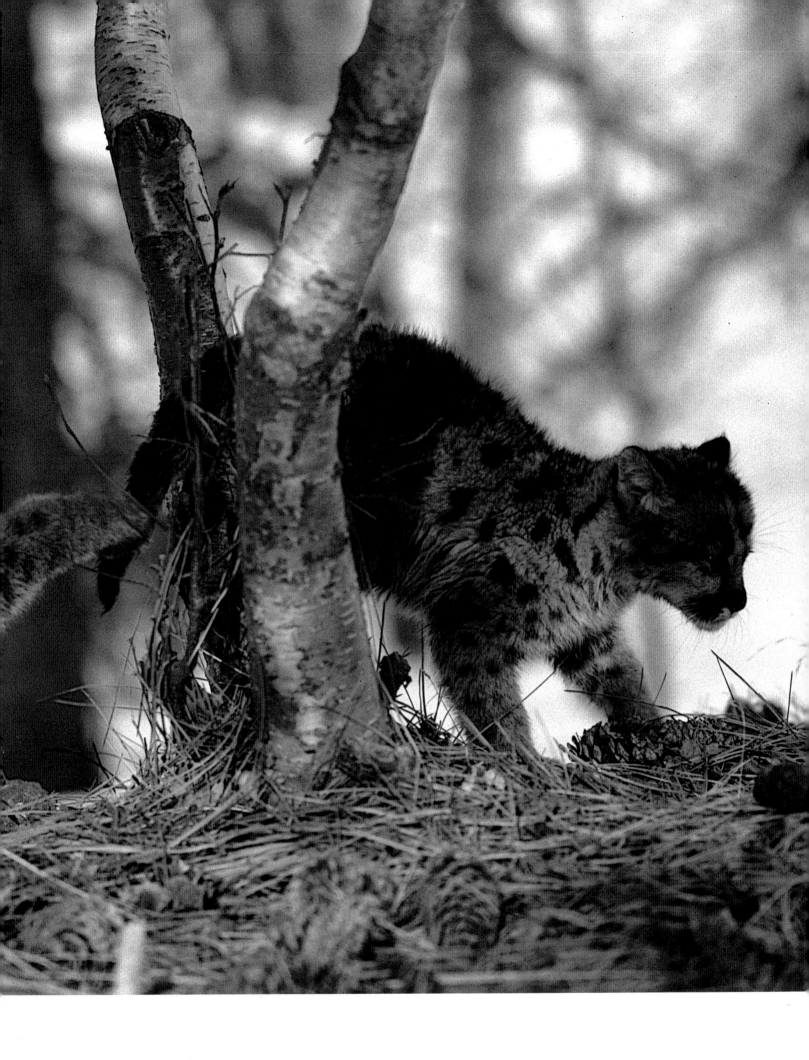

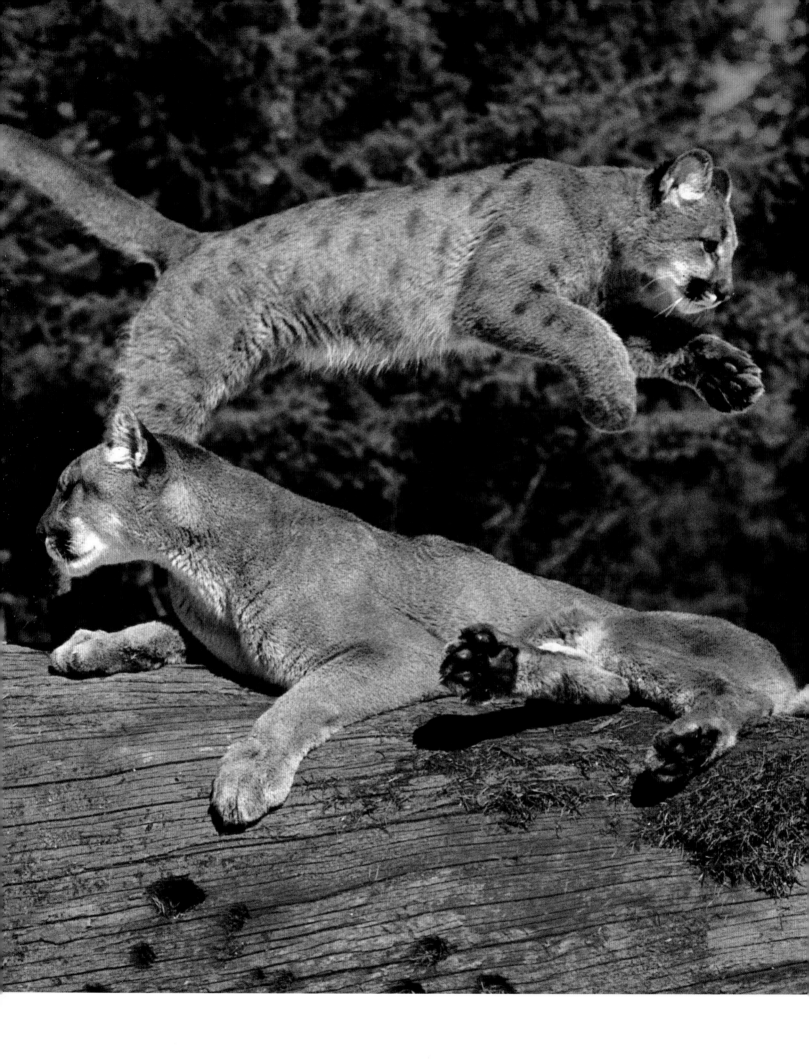

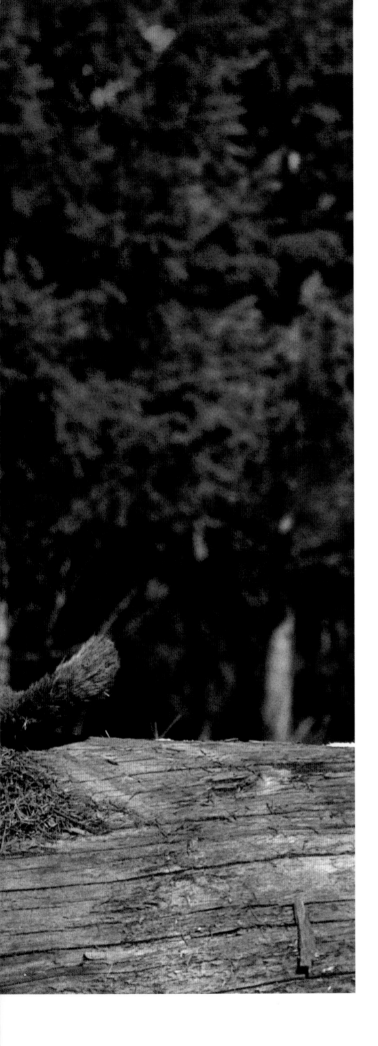

A kitten takes a flying leap over its parent. Tom Walker

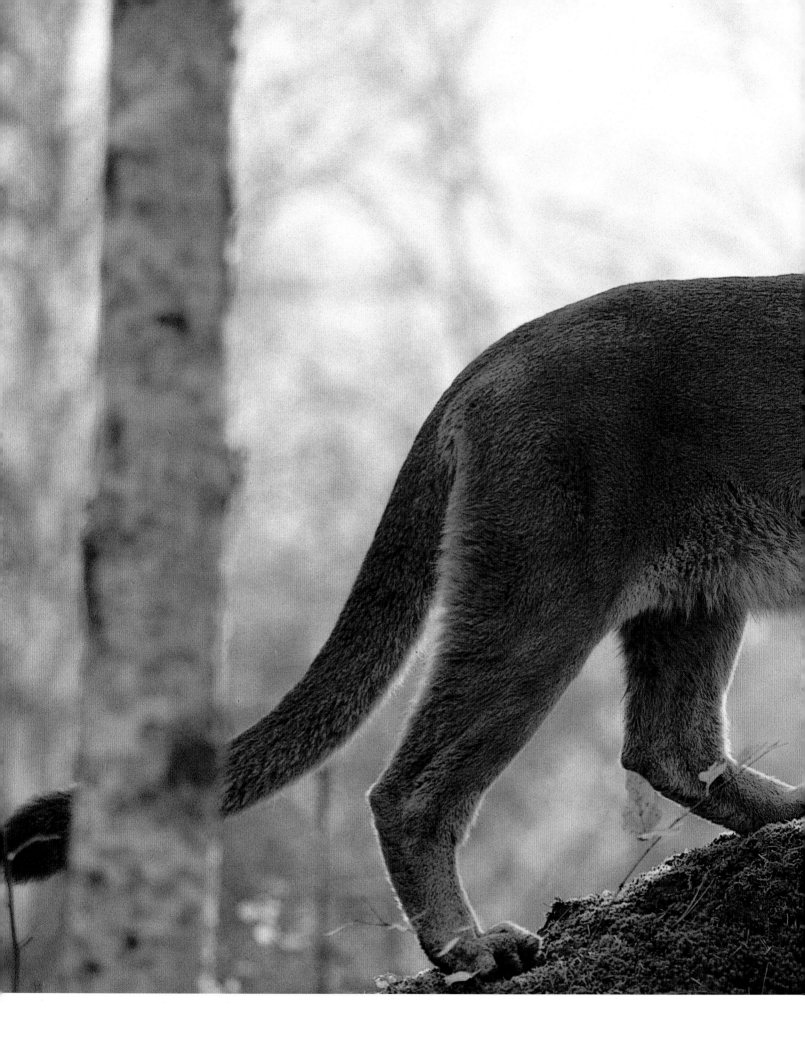

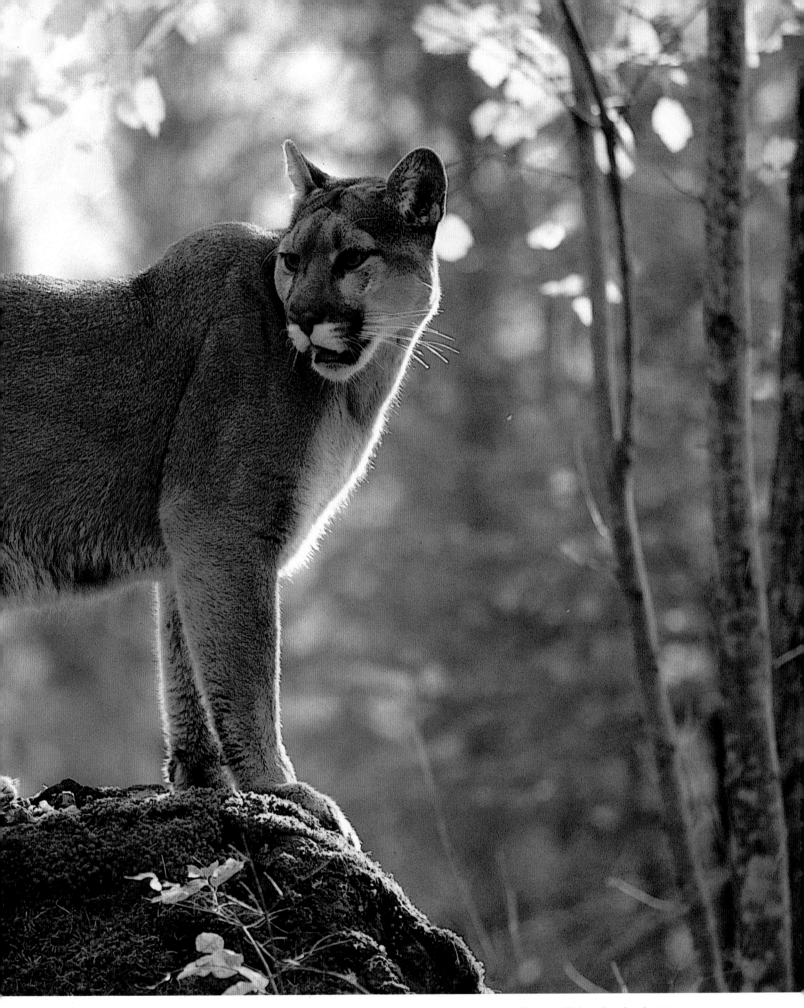

Mountain lions leave their mothers and enter adult life at the age of twelve to twenty-four months. They are likely to live for about ten years—barring accidents or encounters with "sport" hunters. Wayne Lynch

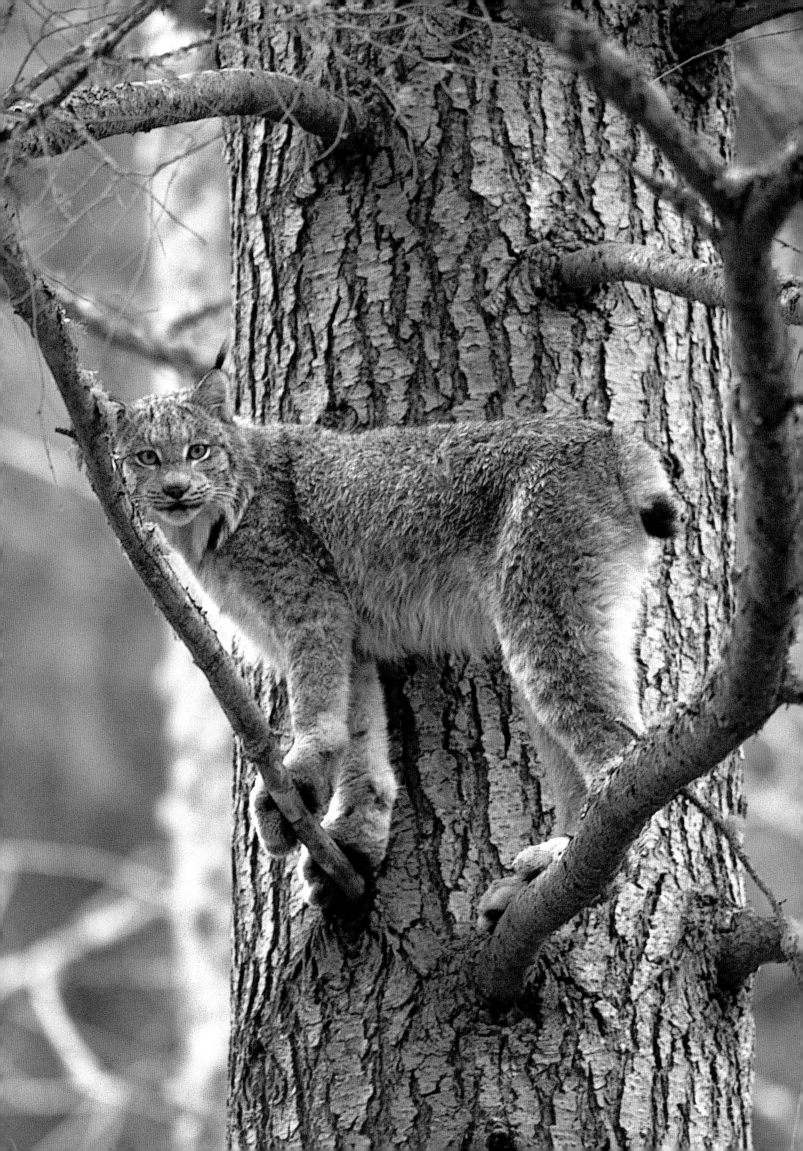

ABUNDANT LIFE

''YOU TAKE MY LIFE WHEN YOU DO TAKE
THE MEANS WHEREBY I LIVE.''

—William Shakespeare,
The Merchant of Venice

There is, as the saying goes, more than one way to kill a cat. Some methods, such as hunting and trapping, are shocking and gory. Others—the disruption of living communities on which wild cats depend—are bloodless and indirect. Are these killings tolerable or are they not? Do they threaten bobcats, lynx or mountain lions with extinction?

Let's take hunting first. In one part or other of their range, bobcats, lynx and mountain lions are all killed for ''sport.'' Whatever the species that is sought, cat hunting is a sweaty, hairy-chested form of entertainment. Ernest Thompson Seton, after scanning thirty years of published accounts on mountain-lion hunting, noted that most stories tell how the hunter, ''absolutely alone and without assistance of any kind, excepting that given by a pack of Cougar hounds and a very small army of experienced mountaineers, and armed with practically nothing but two or three high-power repeating rifles, had actually done to death a gigantic, ferocious, roaring, yelling Cougar that, according to the most conservative guesses, weighed when alive over 300 pounds and was estimated to be 11 feet long.''

Although mountain-lion hunting is steadily losing its allure, it is still permitted and practised in all the western provinces and states, wherever lions exist in reasonable numbers. With one exception: in California, the sport was

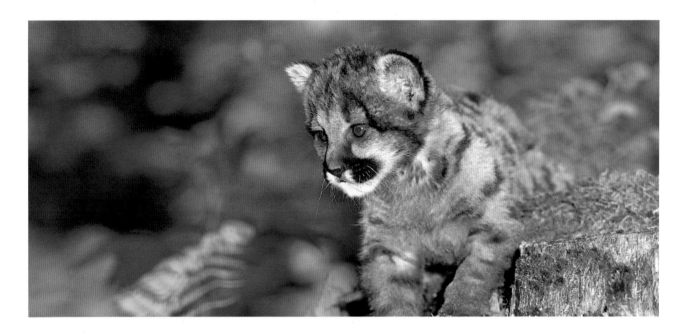

Because the death of a female mountain lion implies the loss of her present and future kittens, it is especially important to limit the number of females that are shot. Under careful management, the hunting season will be closed when a specified number of females have been killed. Thomas Kitchin

recently outlawed by a state-wide plebiscite. In fact, mountain-lion hunting has been prohibited in California for most of the past thirty years, since the old pest-control bounty ended in the early 1960s. The protection was only revoked in 1986, when the demands of sportsmen and ranchers overrode the protests of environmental and animal-welfare advocates. The controversy over this decision opened the way for skirmishing in the courts and, in 1990, for a public debate and vote.

The issue appeared on the ballot paper as Proposition 117, the California Wildlife Protection Act. Amongst other things, this measure advocated a permanent ban on mountain-lion hunting—a straightforward proposal that called for a straightforward yes or no. But in the weeks that led up to voting day, it became clear that this apparently simple question could be framed in radically different ways by radically different people. For those who supported hunting, the key concern was to ensure the "wise use" of a valued natural resource. For them, the question was (to borrow the words of a California Fish

and Game report), "Is the consumptive use of the mountain lion resource appropriate?" And their reply was "Yes, of course." With a population that, by the best scientific estimates, stood at 5,100 or more, the state Fish and Game department concluded, quite reasonably, that the cats could sustain a limited annual "take" of twenty to sixty individuals. According to an article in the hunters' magazine *Outdoor Life*, a ban on the sport hunting of mountain lions would serve no useful purpose and would turn the species into "a free-roaming museum specimen instead of a functioning, contributing natural resource."

The people in the anti-hunting camp did not buy these arguments. For them the central concern was the preservation of the Earth's vanishing wildness. In the words of the Mountain Lion Preservation Foundation (now the Mountain Lion Foundation, based in Sacramento), the mountain lion is "our last great predator, challenging us to live in harmony with nature." Should these animals be shot for fun? Most emphatically not. For one thing, the opponents of hunting said, again quite reasonably, the scientists' population figures were educated guesses, freehand extrapolations based on small fragments of data. What if their estimates were incorrect? For another, hunting pressure might well add to the stress caused by loss of living space—a very real concern in a state where the human population has topped 30 million and where some 2 million hectares (5 million acres) of wildlife range have been destroyed in the past half century. In the words of *Dances with Wolves* author Michael Blake, "Each citizen joining the struggle to save the mountain lion and its way of life gives back to a country from which too much has already been taken—America."

The mountain-lion protectors had another objection to the hunters' form of entertainment. They thought it was perverted. What kind of person would get his kicks by chasing a cat with a pack of hounds, running it up a tree and shooting it off a branch? What was the point of killing a magnificent animal just to take its hide or head as a trophy? When the votes were counted, the anti-hunt faction had won, and mountain-lion hunting was again outlawed in California. The passage of the act also promised $30 million a year for thirty years to purchase wildlife habitat.

Meanwhile, a similar tug-of-war was, and is, being enacted in western Europe, in a contest that is less public but far more perilous. There the issue is the "sport" hunting of lynx, in a region where the cats are either rare or locally extinct. In Switzerland, for example, there are only about one hundred of the "superpredators." Yet an informal opinion poll shows that a small minority of people (less than 15 per cent) believe that the cats should continue to be protected. The majority are about evenly split between those who want the lynx classified as a

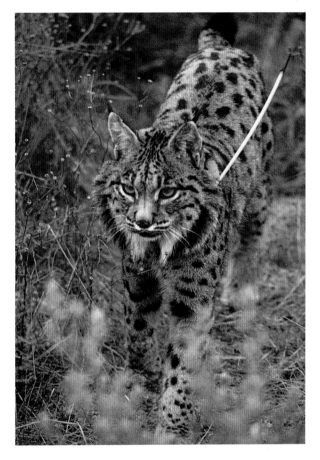

The remnant and reintroduced lynx populations in France, Switzerland, Spain and other parts of western Europe suffer heavy losses to illegal hunting and trapping. This photograph shows a Spanish lynx that has temporarily been fitted with a radio collar and antenna as part of research to assist with the animal's conservation. Nano Cañas

noxious predator and those who think it should be listed as a "game" animal. In Sweden, where lynx persisted in good numbers to the 1960s, they have recently been reduced to a small remnant by overhunting. Perhaps Europe should be looking to California for more than EuroDisney.

But if Europeans sometimes seem careless of their own wild cats, they can be passionate defenders of animals in other parts of the world (a tendency that many of us will recognize in ourselves—if uncomfortable changes have to be made, we hope it will be somewhere else). The campaign against fur-trapping, for example, has many adherents on both sides of the Atlantic, and cats again are a special focus of interest and concern. It is not by chance that a large British campaign, which has been honoured by the British Veterinary Association for its dedication to "putting fur out of fashion," works under the name and emblem of LYNX.

As George Orwell put it, "All animals are created equal, but some animals are created more equal than others." In human eyes, lynx are more equal than most. They have a special power to turn people against the fur trade. It was a lynx that brought about the conversion of Ernest Thompson Seton ("To this day," he wrote twenty years after the fact, "I cannot forget the kitten-like wonder of those big, mild eyes, turned on me as I fired."). It was a lynx that got through to Anahareo, Grey Owl's wife and the person who persuaded him to turn from trapping to conservation. The last lynx she trapped "had gnawed at his paw until the bones were bare of flesh." It was a lynx that moved trapper Frank Conibear to invent a quick-kill, "humane" trap that is all too gradually being put into use by the fur industry.

A lynx lives longer when caught in a trap than any other animal [Conibear observed in a 1946 pamphlet called "Testimony of a Trapper"]. I have known two to live for three weeks in traps and be alive when I got there, but they were very, very thin. The feet of the lynx are so large that unless it steps fairly in the middle of the trap, it is caught by only one or two toes and, as the days go by, the jaws of the trap squeeze tighter till they separate the joints of the bone. Sometimes the sudden jerks of the lynx break the last shred and it is free. By that time, the whole of the caught foot is usually frozen, so the lynx must die from a rotten foot. Of all the deaths caused by trapping, I think that from a foot thawing out and rotting out is the most awful.

The suffering of trapped animals is the heart of the anti-fur campaign, but it is certainly not the movement's only concern. The history of the fur trade, in the words of a LYNX brochure, "is a tragic and continuing story of the decline and disappearance of many of the world's most magnificent animals": sea mink, ocelots, tigers, snow leopards. Anti-fur activists worry that "wild animal populations cannot withstand the heavy losses" inflicted on them by the fur industry—losses that, until very recently, have been at all-time highs. According to a report published by the Ontario (Canada) Trappers Association, an average of almost 19 million wild animals was "harvested" by North American trappers during each year of the early 1980s, or almost four times as many as in the same decade of the previous century. (The trade has declined sharply since 1988.)

On the face of it, the anti-trapping movement seems to have cornered the market on both reason and righteousness. ("Join the moral majority," LYNX urges.) But fur-trade supporters have their own reasons for pride. They can point

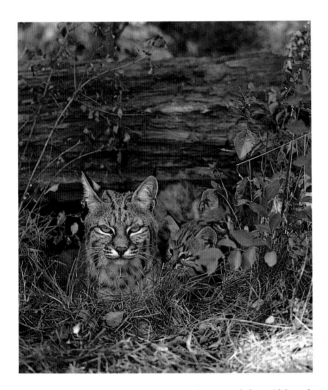

A female bobcat guards her kittens at their natal den. Although bobcats weathered the intense trapping of the 1980s, their survival owed as much to luck as to good management. We still lack reliable ways to determine safe "harvests." In particular, we need a cheap, accurate method for estimating the populations of these hard-to-see-and-census wild cats. Alan & Sandy Carey

to the progress they have made in trapper education and trap research, which help to reduce the suffering of furbearing animals. They can show how trapping helps to maintain endangered human cultures by permitting aboriginal people to live on the land and retain contact with their ancestral way of life (about half of Canadian trappers are of native ancestry). And they can justifiably conclude, with the Ontario trappers' report, that "furbearing populations [in North America] are generally not threatened by

harvesting," even at today's high volumes. A properly managed fur trade does not mean certain doom.

For evidence, we need look no farther than to bobcats. Until the mid-1970s, bobcats scarcely figured in the fur industry. On a good day, a prime pelt might go for ten dollars. Then, in 1973, a series of meetings in Washington, D.C., began to change everything, when representatives of eighty countries drafted an agreement called CITES, the Convention on International Trade in Endangered Species of Wild Fauna and Flora. Its purpose was a noble one: to prevent commercial exploitation of animals and plants that were threatened with extinction. Among the first species to go on the prohibited list, known as Appendix I, were leopards, cheetahs, jaguars and other cats that were being hunted into oblivion to satisfy a fad for spotted garments. Fashion buyers responded to this ban by searching the world for alternatives. They found them in the Americas, where a variety of spotted and dotted cat pelts could be obtained in large numbers. Three South American species—the ocelot, oncilla and margay—have since ended up on Appendix I because of this shift in demand, and another one, Geoffroy's cat, may be on the way to collapse.

But the feisty little bobcat came through largely unscathed, despite prices that leaped to $300 a pelt and an *annual* death toll of about 94,000 in the late seventies. Much of the credit for their survival goes to the bobcats themselves, which can compensate for heavy losses by producing large litters. But a tip of the hat is also due to the wildlife managers who conducted research, set trapping seasons and bag limits, and otherwise did their best to maintain a "sustainable harvest." Their methods were far from rigorous, a fact that their opponents never let them forget. In fact, the Defenders of Wildlife managed to block U.S. bobcat exports for several years on the grounds that, with no accurate knowledge of bobcat numbers, the government could not prove that its "harvest" limits were safe—a proof that CITES required. Eventually the laws were changed to accept the "best available information" rather than hard-and-fast proof as the basis for management. Whatever its imperfections, this system seems to have worked, because the bobcat has survived in very healthy numbers —between 700,000 and 1,500,000 in the United States alone.

Obviously, heavy trapping does not inevitably tend to extinction, as the anti-fur lobby contends. The North American fur trade is entitled to its boast that it has never forced a species into oblivion. But this does not mean it never causes harm. Just as you or I can be sick without reaching death's doorstep, so a species can be reduced in numbers without being in danger of utter disappearance. This, despite the fur trade's best attempts at management, is what has happened recently to lynx in North America.

Again, the story begins with a whim of the garment trade. Around 1970, the czars of fashion decreed that long-haired furs were to be the rage, and the cost of an average lynx pelt leaped from $40 to $400 in the space of a decade. Exceptionally fine furs went for $1,000. Encouraged by these unheard-of prices, trappers went after lynx with a vengeance and, during the seventies, brought about 37,000 pelts per year to market— well over twice the annual rate of the previous decade. Through the ups and downs of the lynx-and-hare cycle, the demand was relentless.

We know now that lynx cannot withstand such an unceasing assault. In particular, they should not be heavily trapped during a cyclic trough. The lynx that survive the lean years are the "seed" for the large populations that develop after the hares come back. But with the high prices and lax regulations of the 1970s, too many lynx were killed when the animals were scarce. This left too few to give birth to a resurgence. As a result, peak populations in 1981 and 1991 were both badly depressed. In the province of Alberta, Canada, for example, about 23,000 lynx were trapped in the peak year of the 1970s, 14,000 at the corresponding point in the 1980s, and fewer than 3,000 in the early 1990s, although more or less comparable effort was put into catching them. While not exactly endangered, lynx had suffered a drastic loss, not just in Alberta but also in Alaska and the other Canadian provinces.

As soon as fur managers noticed the slump, they responded with education programs, quotas, reduced seasons and, in some places, outright closures, especially during the low years of the lynx cycle. For the most part, these restrictions have held despite political pressure from cash-strapped trappers, who mourn for their lost income. Yet even with strict management, Alberta lynx expert Arlen Todd (the person who first documented the problem) believes that it will be several decades before lynx regain their normal abundance in most of Canada.

As worrisome as this story is, it is also strangely satisfying. For one thing, the moral is clear (killing too many animals is not a good thing), and solutions emerge easily (kill fewer lynx). For another, it is easy to tell who the Bad Guys are (the garment industry, trappers, fur traders). But best of all, it seems that the Good

Guys are nice folks like us—people who care about animals and who would never be so misguided as to believe that furs could be "fun." We have the pleasure of feeling outraged and smug.

Sad to say, we are not entitled to this self-satisfaction. The fact is that, without so much as seeing a fur, we have all contributed to the lynx's misfortune. Although overtrapping was driven by the market for furs, it was made possible by logging and mineral exploration, which have opened the northern forest to an ever-branching, outward-reaching network of roads and cutlines. Wherever the trails have led, trappers have soon moved in. In the past, when access to timber was more limited, trapping was restricted to the reach of the few existing roads. These limited areas were surrounded by large expanses of closed forest that served as refuges for lynx and supplied a steady flow of animals to replace those that were harvested. In the far northern territories of Canada where few roads have yet been made, this method of replenishment continues to operate. There and only there, lynx populations have held their own against the downward trend. But in Alaska and the provinces, the unofficial lynx refuges have now been sacrificed to the search for metals, minerals, petroleum and pulpwood to enhance our way of life.

Our unwitting collaboration with the fur industry is not the end of our complicity. As members of industrial, demand-driven societies, we have also contributed to the lynx's decline significantly, if subtly, in ways that have not spilled a single drop of blood. Every time we use a piece of paper or take shelter in a wooden house, we benefit from a system that values the lynx's forests not for their ability to support wild cats, nor even as a source of furs, but simply as a means of supplying wood products. The goal of this system is to grow logs as a crop, by maximizing the production of saleable trees and by minimizing the time between successive cuts. The more efficiently we do this—the more we simplify the forests and use their growing power to meet our narrowly defined purposes—the harder it becomes for lynx (and many other creatures) to survive.

Lynx need two kinds of forest habitat to live comfortably: dense patches of gnarly, tangled mature forest for shelter and birth-dens, and lush, juicy meadows and young woods where they can hunt for hares. What's more, they need a patchy pattern of forest types, in which young and old growth are interspersed. The wood trade, on the other hand, does not particularly value mature forest. From its point of view, old forest is "decadent," or overripe, and the blowdowns and fallen logs that provide shelter to lynx represent nothing but wasted profits. The young forests that feed snowshoe hares are also undesirable because they are preproductive; they need to be hurried along towards a maximal cut." This is done through standard farming techniques such as weeding and thinning—manipulations that leave hares with little to eat. Finally, very large cutting operations, which may be desirable for efficiency, destroy the mosaic of forest types that lynx, and most other large animals, need.

Under natural conditions, when timber is not being cropped, the patchwork of the forest is as random as wildfire, which creates an ever-changing pattern of different plants of different ages. By dedicating the forest to the commercial production of trees, we have cast fire as a public enemy. To us, burning a forest is like burning money. But to rabbits, deer and wild cats, a forest fire is an investment that will pay in future growth. While a new burn is of little value to humans or wildlife, the lush young forest that grows up within the first fifteen to fifty years after a blaze spreads a banquet for plant-eaters and, ultimately, for their predators. Although clear-cutting can be used to initiate the same process, the cutblocks are often too large and the regeneration too hurried to create an optimal lynx forest.

"I feel strongly that suppressing forest fires over huge areas and rushing logged forests through their early stages—precisely the stages that are most productive of hares—has resulted in low populations of lynx," says biologist David Hatler, author of the lynx management strategy of the British Columbia Ministry of the Environment. Though these effects cannot be quantified, Hatler believes the wood industry has caused the animals more harm than has trapping.

Like so much else in the forest, the losses caused by timber extraction have generally not been sensed. The scientific literature, which annually consumes a small forest itself to convey truths great and small, has so far published one five-page article on lynx and "forest management." Scarcely more attention has been paid to the effects of logging on mountain lions, bobcats or, for that matter, most other forest creatures (except for the few that are most desired by human hunters). If forests are glorified tree farms, animals do not matter.

But if forests are to be forests, then everything is important. Every component, living and non-living, plays a role in maintaining the cyclic connections that keep the forest whole. Air, soil, rain and fire. Mineral, vegetable and animal. Soil mites and earthworms, grouse and ovenbirds, hares and deer, bobcats and mountain lions. Meadows, young woods and dark old growth, in the ever-changing green-on-green of nature's slow kaleidoscope. Seen and unseen, everything matters here.

Can we hope to have healthy forests, with a full abundance of life, and still enjoy some of the comfort and wealth that the modern wood trade provides? In some places, especially where forests have been reduced to tree plantations, it is already too late. But where logging pressure has been less destructive, there is still room for hope. Speaking again of lynx in his home province, David Hatler concludes that "It is probably not too late to integrate forestry and lynx management in much of northern British Columbia, but it certainly is about time."

What is needed, Hatler and others contend, is a "new forestry," in which maintaining the diversity of life in the forest is part of our conscious intention. By studying natural forests and trying to imitate them with our logging practices, we stand a chance of conserving cats and other wildlife in their natural abundance. The specifics of this practice are still being worked out—varying cutblock sizes, retaining dead trees and blow-downs in logged areas, protecting areas of old-growth forest, and so on—and are being implemented by a few forward-thinking companies.

Still, it has to be admitted that our knowledge of what the forest needs is shockingly limited. "You've got to crawl before you can walk," David Hatler says. "When it comes to maintaining biodiversity in our forests, we've just learned to crawl. Now we have to get up and run a marathon."

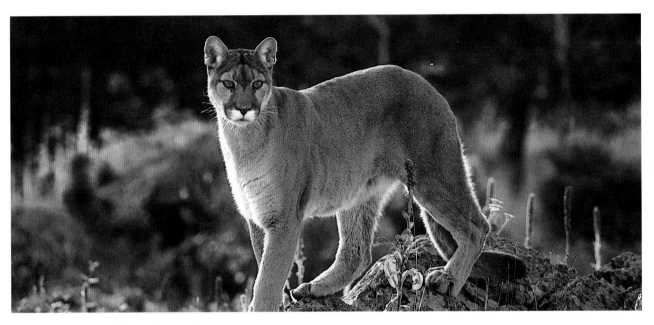

Although little is known about the effects of logging on mountain lions, recent research suggests that the cats steer clear of areas where people are active, even if the forest is otherwise habitable. They also appear to avoid clearcuts for about six years after the loggers have gone. Alan & Sandy Carey

Overleaf: *The future of lynx, bobcats and mountain lions depends on our willingness to share the Earth with them.*
Alan & Sandy Carey

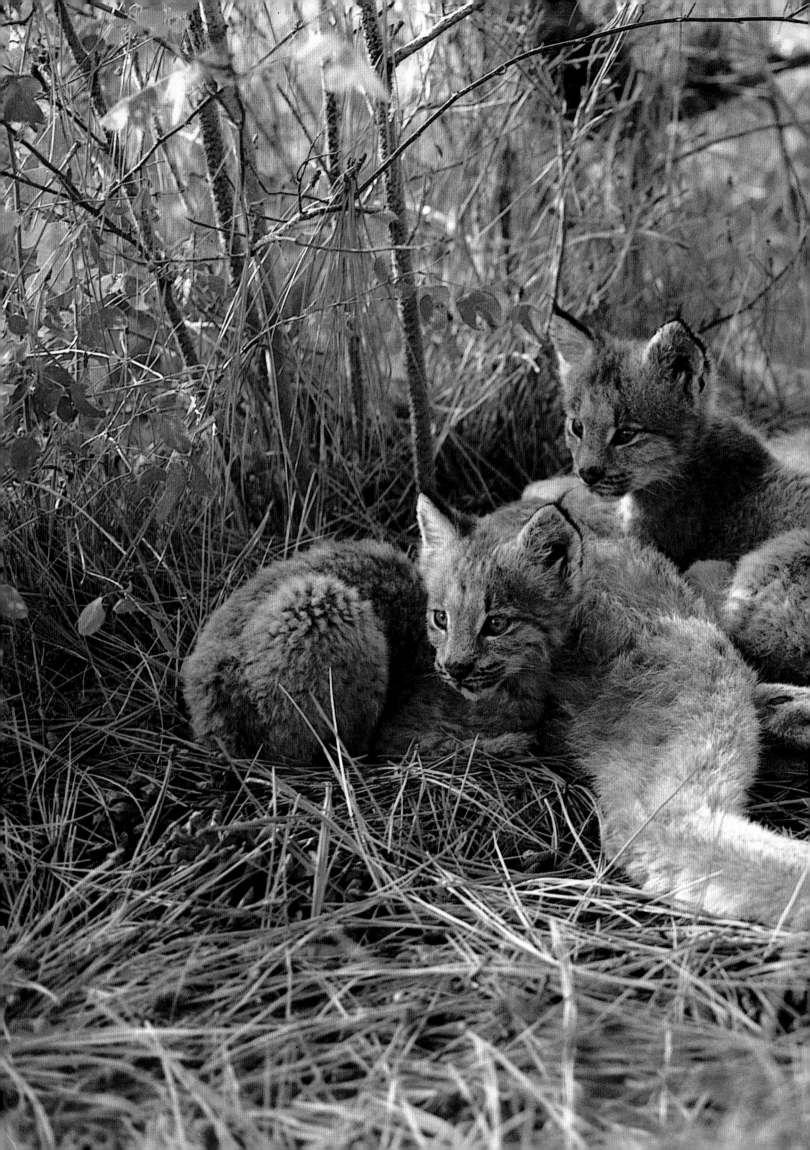

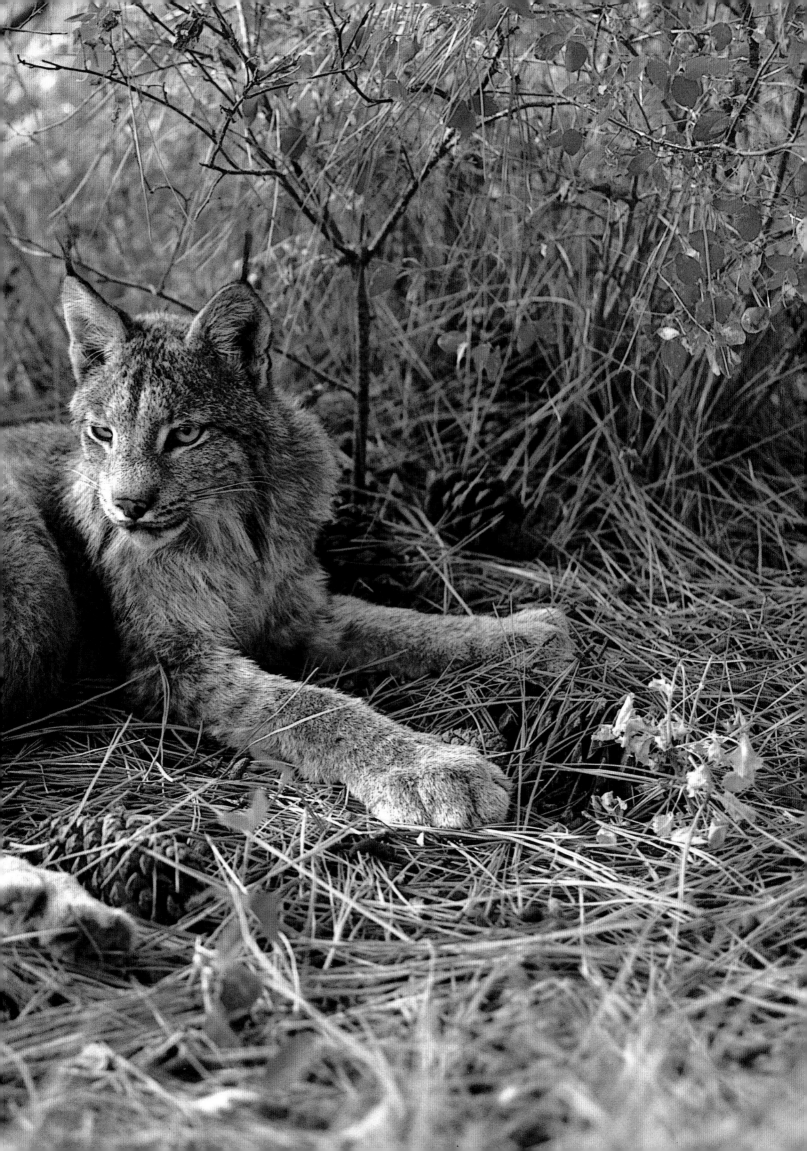

REFERENCES

In addition to the sources listed below, the author benefited from correspondence and discussions with Knut Atkinson and David Hatler of the British Columbia Ministry of the Environment, Stan Boutin of the University of Alberta, David Gladders of the Fur Institute of Canada, Daryll Hebert of Alberta Pacific Forest Industries, Paul Galbraith of Parks Canada, Martin Jalkotzy and Ian Ross of the Alberta Cougar Project, Kim Poole of the Northwest Territories Department of Renewable Resources, John Seidensticker of the Smithsonian Institution, Brian Slough of the Yukon Department of Renewable Resources, and Blair Rippin, Richard Quinlan and Arlen Todd of Alberta Forestry Lands and Wildlife.

General

Kitchener, Andrew. 1991. *The natural history of the wild cats*. Ithaca, N.Y.: Comstock.

Seidensticker, John, and Lumpkin, Susan, eds. 1991. *Great cats: majestic creatures of the wild*. Emmaus, Penn.: Rodale Press.

Seton, Ernest Thompson. 1953 [1909]. *Lives of game animals: cats, wolves and foxes*. Boston: Charles T. Branford.

Lynx and Bobcats

Anderson, Eric M. 1987. *A critical review and annotated bibliography of literature on the bobcat*. Colorado Division of Wildlife Special Report No. 62.

Bailey, Theodore N. 1981. Factors of bobcat social organization and some management implications. *Worldwide Furbearer Conference Proceedings*, pp. 984-1000.

———. 1974. Social organization in a bobcat population. *Journal of Wildlife Management* 38: 435-46.

Bailey, Theodore N., et al. 1986. An apparent overexploited lynx population on the Kenai Peninsula, Alaska. *Journal of Wildlife Management* 50 (2): 279-90.

Brand, Christopher J., and Keith, Lloyd B. 1979. Lynx demography during a snowshoe hare decline in Alberta. *Journal of Wildlife Management* 43: 827-49.

Brand, Christopher J., et al. 1976. Lynx responses to changing snowshoe hare densities in central Alberta. *Journal of Wildlife Management* 40: 416-28.

Breitenmoser, Urs, and Haller, Heinrich. 1987. La réintroduction du lynx (*Lynx lynx* L 1758): une appréciation après 15 ans d'expérience en Suisse. *Ciconia* 11: 119-30.

DeStefano, Stephen. 1987. The lynx. In *Audubon wildlife report*, pp. 410-22. Orlando, Florida: Academic Press.

Fox, John F. 1978. Forest fires and the snowshoe hare-Canada lynx cycle. *Oecologia* 31: 349-74.

Gluesing, Ernest A., et al. 1986. Management of the North American bobcat: information needs for nondetriment findings. *Transactions North America Wildlife and Natural Resources Conference* 51: 183-92.

Hatler, David F. 1988. A lynx management strategy for British Columbia. B.C. Ministry of Environment Wildlife Bulletin No. B-60.

Herrenschmidt, Véronique. 1990. Le lynx: un cas de réintroduction de superprédateur. *Revue d'écologie: la terre et la vie* 5: 159-74.

Istchenko, Vic (producer). 1992. *The rise and fall of Yukon lynx*, an hour-long video from Northern Native Broadcasting, Whitehorse, Yukon.

Jackson, Dewaine H., and Jackson, Laura S. 1987. An observation of fighting between free-ranging bobcats, *Lynx rufus. Canadian Field-Naturalist* 101: 465-66.

Jonsson, Stefan. 1986. Projekt Ldjur [Lynx project]. *Fauna och Flora* 81: 165-66.

Keith, Lloyd B., and Windberg, Lamar A. 1978. A demographic analysis of the snowshoe hare cycle. *Wildlife Monographs* 58.

Knick, Steven T. 1990. Ecology of bobcats relative to exploitation and a prey decline in southeastern Idaho. *Wildlife Monographs* 108.

Knowles, Pamela R. 1985. Home range size and habitat selection of bobcats, *Lynx rufus*, in north-central Montana. *Canadian Field-Naturalist* 99: 6-12.

Koehler, Gary. 1988. Bobcat bill of fare. *Natural History* 97 (December): 48-57.

1987. The bobcat. *Audubon wildlife report*, pp. 399-426. Orlando, Florida: Academic Press.

Koehler, Gary M., and Brittell, J. David. 1990. Managing spruce-fir habitat for lynx and snowshoe hares. *Journal of Forestry* 88 (10): 10-14.

Maehr, David S., and Brady, James R. 1986. Food habits of bobcats in Florida. *Journal of Mammalogy* 67: 133-38.

McCord, Chet M., and Cardoza, James E. 1982. Bobcat and lynx. In *Wild mammals of North America*, ed. Chapman, J. A., and Feldhamer, G. A. Baltimore: Johns Hopkins.

Mingozzi, Toni, et al. 1988. Dati storici sulla presenza della lince, *Lynx lynx* (L), nell'Italia nord-occidentale. *Supplemente alle Richerche di Biologia della Selvaggina* 14 (1): 479-500.

Monthey, Roger W. 1986. Responses of snowshoe hares, *Lepus americanus*, to timber harvesting in northern Maine. *Canadian Field-Naturalist* 100 (4): 568-70.

Palomares, F., et al. 1991. The status and distribution of the Iberian lynx *Felis pardina* (Temminck) in Coto Doñana area, SW Spain. *Biological Conservation* 57: 159-169.

Parker, G. R. 1983. The ecology of the lynx (*Lynx canadensis*) on Cape Breton Island. *Canadian Journal of Zoology* 61: 770-86.

———. 1981. Winter habitat use and hunting activities of lynx (*Lynx canadensis*) on Cape Breton Island, Nova Scotia. *Worldwide Furbearer Conference Proceedings*, pp. 211-48.

Poole, Kim. 1991. Lynx research in the NWT, 1990-91. Northwest Territories Renewable Resources Manuscript Report No. 52.

Quinn, Norman W. S., and Thompson, John E. 1987. Dynamics of an exploited Canada lynx population in Ontario. *Journal of Wildlife*

Management 51 (2): 297-305.

Ragni, Bernardino. 1988. Status e problemi di conservazione dei felidi (*Felidae*) in Italia. *Supplemente alle Richerche di Biologia della Selvaggina* 14 (1): 455-77.

Todd, Arlen W. 1985. The Canada lynx: ecology and management. *Canadian Trapper* 13 (2): 15-20.

Toweill, Dale E., and Anthony, Robert G. 1988. Annual diet of bobcats in Oregon's Cascade Range. *Northwest Science* 62: 99-103.

Tumlison, Renn. 1987. Felis lynx. *Mammalian Species* 269: 1-8.

Tumlison, Renn, and McDaniel, V. Rick. 1990. Analysis of the fall and winter diet of the bobcat in eastern Arkansas. *Proceedings Arkansas Academy of Science* 44: 114-16.

Turbak, Gary. 1988. Shy survivor. *National Wildlife* 26 (December/January): 12-16.

———. 1985. A tale of two cats. *International Wildlife* 15 (2): 4-11.

Vourch'h, Anne. 1990. Représentation de l'animal et perceptions sociales de sa réintroduction. Le cas du lynx des Vosges. *Revue d'écologie: la terre et la vie* 5: 175-87.

Ward, R. M. P., and Krebs, C. J. 1985. Behavioural responses of lynx to declining snowshoe hare abundance. *Canadian Journal of Zoology* 63: 2817-24.

Williams, Richard D. 1990. Bobcat electrocutions on powerlines. *California Fish and Game* 76: 187-89.

Williams, Ted. 1989. The bobcat. *Country Journal* 16 (March/April): 86-90.

Mountain Lions

Anderson, Allen E. 1983. *A critical review of literature on puma* (felis concolor). Colorado Division of Wildlife Special Report No. 54.

Bartmann, Richard M., et al. 1992. Compensatory mortality in a Colorado mule deer population. *Wildlife Monographs* 121.

Belden, Robert C. 1988. The Florida panther. *Audubon Wildlife Report*, pp. 515-32. Orlando, Florida: Academic Press.

Fegus, Chuck. 1991. The Florida panther verges on extinction. *Science* 251: 1178-80.

Flowers, Charles. 1989. Searching for the one true cat. *National Wildlife* 27: 24-28.

Gerson, Helen B. 1988. Cougar, *Felis concolor*, sightings in Ontario. *Canadian Field-Naturalist* 102: 419-24.

Glass, Kathy. 1987. Lions—mountain or mounted? *Sierra* 72 (July/August): 12-13.

Greenwell, J. R. 1989. The eastern puma: evidence continues to build. *International Society of Cryptozoology Newsletter* 8 (3): 1-8.

Hines, Tommy C., et al. 1987. An overview of panther research and management in Florida. *Proceedings of the Southwestern Nongame Endangered Wildlife Symposium* 3: 140-44.

Hornocker, Maurice G. 1992. Learning to live with mountain lions. *National Geographic* 182(1): 51-65.

———. 1970. An analysis of mountain lion predation upon mule deer and elk in the Idaho Primitive Area. *Wildlife Monographs* 21.

———. 1969. Stalking the mountain lion—to save him. *National Geographic* 89: 638-55.

Laycock, George. 1988. Cougars in conflict. *Audubon* 90: 86-92, 94-95.

Maehr, David S. 1990. The Florida panther and private lands. *Conservation Biology* 4: 167-70.

Maehr, David S., et al. 1990. Food habits of panthers in southwest Florida. *Journal of*

Wildlife Management 54: 420-23.

———. 1989. Early maternal behavior in the Florida panther (*Felis concolor coryi*). *American Midland Naturalist* 122: 34-43.

Mansfield, Terry M. 1986. Mountain lion management in California. *Transactions North American Wildlife and Natural Resources Conference* 51: 178-82.

Mansfield, Terry M., and Weaver, Richard A. 1989. The status of mountain lions in California. *Transactions of the Western Section of the Wildlife Society* 25: 72-76.

Millsap, Brian A., et al. 1990. Setting priorities for the conservation of fish and wildlife species in Florida. *Wildlife Monographs* 111.

Nero, Robert W., and Wrigley, Robert E. 1977. Status and habits of the cougar in Manitoba. *Canadian Field-Naturalist* 91: 28-40.

Parker, G. R. 1983. The eastern cougar in the Maritime provinces. *N.B. Naturalist* 12 (4): 150-55.

Seidensticker, John, and Lumpkin, Susan. 1992. Mountain lions don't stalk people. True or false? *Smithsonian* 22 (February): 113-22.

Seidensticker, John C., et al. 1973. Mountain lion social organization in the Idaho primitive area. *Wildlife Monographs* 35.

Tinsley, Jim Bob. 1987. *The puma: legendary lion of the Americas*. El Paso: Texas Western Press.

Tischendorf, Jay W., ed. 1992. *Eastern panther update* 1 (1): 1-6.

Van Dyke, Fred G., and Brocke, Rainer H. 1987. Sighting and track reports as indices of mountain lion presence. *Wildlife Society Bulletin* 15: 251-56.

Wallace, Joseph. 1986. Has the big cat come back? *Sierra* 71 (May/June): 20-21.

Conservation and Forests

Amory, Cleveland. 1974. *Man kind? our incredible war on wildlife*. New York: Harper and Row.

Barr, B. M., and Braden, K. E. 1988. *The disappearing Russian forest: a dilemma in Soviet resource management*. London: Rowman and Littlefield.

Beebe, Spencer B. 1991. Conservation in temperate and tropical rain forests: the search for an ecosystem approach to sustainability. *Transactions North American Wildlife and Natural Resources Conference* 56: 595-603.

Brown, Lester, et al. 1990. *State of the world 1990: a Worldwatch Institute report on progress toward a sustainable society*. New York: W. W. Norton.

———. 1992. *State of the world 1992: a Worldwatch Institute report on progress toward a sustainable society*. New York: W. W. Norton.

Darr, David D., and Mills, Thomas J. 1991. Trends in timber demands and supplies: implications for resource management in the 21st century. *Transactions North American Wildlife and Natural Resources Conference* 56: 604-12.

Eastman, Don S., et al. 1991. Silviculturists and wildlife habitat managers: competitors or cooperators? *Transactions North American Wildlife and Natural Resources Conference* 56: 640-51.

Ehrlich, Paul, and Ehrlich, Anne. 1981. *Extinction: the causes and consequences of the disappearance of species*. New York: Random House.

Fitzgerald, Sarah. 1989. *International wildlife trade: whose business is it?* Washington, D.C.: World Wildlife Fund.

Fur Institute of Canada. 1986. With respect to the history of the fur trade. Toronto: Fur Institute of Canada.

Hammond, Herb. 1991. *Seeing the forest among the trees: the case for wholistic forest use.* Vancouver: Polestar Press.

Hansen, A. J., et al. 1991. Conserving biodiversity in managed forests: lessons from natural forests. *BioScience* 41 (6): 382-92.

Harris, Larry D. 1984. *The fragmented forest: island biogeography theory and the preservation of biotic diversity.* Chicago: University of Chicago Press.

Hummel, Monte, and Pettigrew, Sherry. 1991. *Wild hunters: predators in peril.* Toronto: Key Porter.

Hunter, Malcolm L., Jr. 1990. *Wildlife, forests, and forestry: principles of managing forests for biological diversity.* Englewood Cliffs, N.J. : Prentice-Hall.

Maini, J. S. 1990. Forests: barometers of environment and economy. In *Planet under stress*, ed. Mungall, C., and McLaren, D. J., pp. 168-87.

Novak, Milan, et al., eds. 1987. *Wild furbearer management and conservation in North America.* Toronto: Ontario Trappers Association and Ontario Ministry of Natural Resources.

O'Brien, Stephen J., and Mayr, Ernest. 1991. Bureaucratic mischief: recognizing endangered species and subspecies. *Science* 251: 1187-88.

Rowe, J. Stan. 1992. The ecosystem approach to forestland management. *Forestry Chronicle* 68 (2): 222-24.

Samson, Fred B., et al. 1991. News perspectives in Alaska forest management. *Transactions North American Wildlife and Natural Resources Conference* 56: 640-51.

Sleeper, Barbara. 1991. Vanishing wild cats. *Animals* (July/August): 24-28.

Spies, Thomas A., et al. 1991. Trends in ecosystem management at the stand level. *Transactions North American Wildlife and Natural Resources Conference* 56: 628-39.

Westman, Walter E. 1990. Managing for biodiversity: unresolved science and policy questions. *BioScience* 40 (1): 26-33.

Williams, Barbara L., and Marcot, Bruce G. 1991. Use of biodiversity indicators for analyzing and managing forest landscapes. *Transactions North American Wildlife and Natural Resources Conference* 56: 613-27.

Williamson, Lonnie. 1990. They're trying to ban hunting in California. *Outdoor Life* 185 (June): 74-82.

Wilson, E. O., ed. 1986. *Biodiversity.* Washington, D.C.: National Academy Press.

INDEX

Aboriginal trappers, 123
Alaska, 124, 125
Alberta, 124
Alberta Cougar Project, 63, 70
Alligator Alley, 70
Alsace, 10
Anahareo, 122
Anti-fur lobby, 122, 124
Appearance. *See* Field marks
Appendix I, CITES, 123
Attacks on people by mountain lions,
    68

Badger, 91
Bavaria, 10
Big Cypress, 81
Blake, Michael, 121
Bobcat, 1, 2, 3, 10, 12-13, 22, 23, 24,
    25, 27, 29, 35, 37, 39, 41, 42, 43,
    45, 47, 49, 50, 51, 53, 55, 56, 57,
    58, 61, 123-24, 126
Bounties, 68, 69, 70, 120. *See also*
    Predator control

Caching prey, 93
California, 68, 119-20
California Wildlife Protection Act, 120
Calls. *See* Vocalizations
Canada, 2, 8, 11, 12, 13, 66, 67, 123,
    124, 125. *See also* individual place
    names
Canada lynx. *See* Lynx, North
    American
Canine teeth, 5, 19
Cape Breton, 13
Captive breeding, 70
Cats: adaptations of, 5, 8, 29, 87;
    hunting strategy of, 5, 8; wild,
    status of, 3, 123. *See also*
    individual species
Cheetah, 75, 123
CITES, 123, 124
Classification. *See* Taxonomy
Claws, 8, 9, 88
Colorado, 39, 107
Communication, 45, 47. *See also* Scent
    marking; Vocalizations
Competition between bobcat and
    lynx, 13

Convention on International Trade in
    Endangered Species, 123, 124
Copulation. *See* Reproduction
Cougar, 66. *See also* Mountain lion
Czechoslovakia, 10

Deer, 10, 12, 31, 43, 79, 91, 93
Defenders of Wildlife, 124
Den sites: bobcat, 29, 57; lynx, 9;
    mountain lion, 101, 109
Diet: bobcat, 12-13, 31, 35, 39, 41;
    lynx, 10, 31; mountain lion, 91,
    93. *See also* Hunting
Distribution. *See* Range

Eastern panther or cougar, 69
Endangered species, 2, 3, 9, 10, 69-70.
    See also Florida panther; Lynx,
    Eurasian
Eurasian lynx. *See* Lynx, Eurasian
Everglades, 81
Evolution, 22, 25, 75. *See also* Cats,
    adaptations of
Eyes and eyesight, 17, 103

Fakahatchee Strand, 70
Feet, 9, 13, 15, 21
Felids. *See* Cats; individual species
Felis concolor, 66. *See also* Mountain
    lion
Felis concolor coryi, 69. *See also* Florida
    panther
Felis concolor couguar, 69. *See also*
    Eastern panther or cougar
Felis lynx, 10. *See also* Lynx
Felis rufus, 10, 27. *See also* Bobcat
Field marks: bobcat, 10, 13, 25, 27;
    lynx, 4, 10, 11, 19, 27; mountain
    lion, 75, 109
Fire, 126
Florida panther, 66, 69-70, 80, 81, 83
Food. *See* Diet
Forest: boreal, 8, 11-12, 125;
    conservation, 2-3, 125-26 fire, 126;
    temperate, 1-2
Forestry and forest industry. *See*
    Logging
France, 2, 9, 10, 121
Fredericton, New Brunswick, 69

Fur, 13, 27
Fur trade, 3, 9, 10, 11, 122-25

Galbraith, Paul, 8
Geese, 12
Geoffroy's cat, 123
Germany, 2, 10
Grey Owl, 122

Habitat: bobcat, 2, 13, 23, 29, 126;
    lynx, 2, 8-9, 15, 22, 23, 31, 125-26;
    mountain lion, 2, 69, 77, 79, 121,
    126. *See also* Range
Hare. *See* Rabbits and hares;
    Snowshoe hare
Hatler, David, 126
Hearing, 23
Home range: bobcat, 39, 42, 49; lynx
    42, 49; mountain lion, 71, 89, 95
Horned lark, 41
Hornocker, Maurice, 70
Hunting: bobcat, 12-13, 35, 37, 38, 39,
    43; feline strategy, 5, 8; lynx, 31,
    32, 33; mountain lion, 86; sport,
    3, 9, 68, 119-21. *See also* Diet; Fur
    trade; Home range

Iberian lynx. *See* Lynx, Iberian
Idaho, 12
Inbreeding, 69
Italy, 9

Jackrabbit, 35
Jaguar, 123
Jalkotzy, Martin, 63, 64-65, 70

Kangaroo rat, 39
Kittens: bobcat, 50, 51, 53, 55, 56, 57,
    58, 61; lynx, 53, 55, 56, 59;
    mountain lion, 99, 101, 103, 105,
    107, 109, 111, 112, 115, 117. *See
    also* Reproduction
Koehler, Gary, 12

Lagomorph. *See* Rabbits and hares
Lawson, John, 67-68
Leopard, 9, 123. *See also* Snow
    leopard
Life span, 59, 117

Lilly, Ben, 69
Lion, 1, 66
Lion, mountain. *See* Mountain lion
Litters. *See* Kittens
Livestock. *See* Predator control
Logging, 125-26
Lynx, 1, 2, 3, 5-12, 15, 17, 19, 21, 22,
    23, 31, 32, 33, 42, 45, 47, 49, 51,
    53, 55, 56, 59, 121, 124-26, 127;
    Eurasian, 1, 9, 10, 19, 21, 22, 31,
    53, 121; Iberian, 9, 10, 121; North
    American, 10-12, 19, 22, 23, 31,
    53, 124-25. *See also* Red lynx
LYNX, 122
Lynx-and-hare cycle, 10-12, 124

Maine, 69
Manitoba, 67
Man-killers, 68
Margay, 123
Marking behaviour. *See* Scent
    marking
Markings. *See* Field marks
Mexico, 12, 67
Mortality. *See* Life span; Sport
    hunting; Trapping
Mountain lion, 1, 2, 3, 62-118, 119-
    121, 126, 127
Mountain Lion Foundation, 120
Mule deer, 93
Muskrat, 41

Native trappers, 123
Netherlands, 2
New forestry, 126
North American lynx. *See* Lynx,
    North American
North Temperate Zone, 1

Ocelot, 3, 122, 123
Old World lynx. *See* Lynx, Eurasian
Oncilla, 123
Ontario Trappers Association, 122,
    123

Panther, 66, 69. *See also* Florida
    panther; Mountain lion
Parker, Gerry, 13

Paws. *See* Claws; Feet; Tracks
Pennsylvania, 67
Play, 41, 56, 58, 111, 112, 115
Plucking prey, 93
Population: bobcat, 3, 124; lynx, 3, 9-
    11, 121, 124-25; mountain lion, 3,
    67, 120
Portugal, 2
Predator control, 3, 9, 12, 68-69, 70
Prince Albert National Park, 8
Proposition 117, 120
Puma, 66. *See also* Mountain lion
Purring, 55, 105. *See also* Vocalizations

Rabbits and hares, 10-13, 31, 35, 91.
    See also Snowshoe hare
Radio-collaring, 63, 70, 71, 121
Range: bobcat, 1, 6-7, 12, 13, 22;
    lynx, 1, 6-7, 9-10, 13, 22; mountain
    lion, 1, 64-65, 67-69, 79, 80. *See
    also* Habitat; Home range
Red lynx, 27
Refuges for lynx, 125
Reintroductions, 9-10. *See also* Captive
    breeding
Reproduction: bobcat, 13, 49, 51;
    lynx 11, 49, 51; mountain lion, 69,
    71, 95, 97, 98, 99. *See also* Den
    sites; Kittens; Social organization
Ring hunt, 68
Road building, 125
Ross, Ian, 70
Russia, 2

Salmon River Mountains, 12
Saskatchewan, 8, 67
Scent marking, 42, 47, 49, 95
Schmidt, Ralph, 70
Schwartz, Black Jack, 68
Senses, 17, 24
Seton, Ernest Thompson, 10, 23, 63,
    119, 122
Sex. *See* Reproduction
Sheep River, 63, 70
Shoemaker, Col. H. W., 67, 68
Smell. *See* Scent marking
Snow leopard, 3, 122
Snowshoe hare, 10-12, 31, 91

Social organization, 42, 49, 95, 97. *See
    also* Home range; Reproduction
South America, 1, 67
Spain, 9, 22, 121. *See also* Lynx,
    Iberian
Sport hunting, 3, 9, 68,119-21
Status. *See* Endangered species;
    Population; Cats, wild, status of
Sustainable harvest, 120, 123-24
Sweden, 121
Switzerland, 9, 10, 121

Taxonomy, 1, 10
Teeth, 5, 19
Temperate forest. *See* Forest,
    temperate
Ten-year cycle, 10-12, 124
Territoriality. *See* Home range; Social
    organization
Texas, 12
Thor, 71
Tiger, 1, 3, 122
Todd, Arlen, 124
Tracks, 9, 71
Trapping. *See* Fur trade

United States, 2, 13, 23, 67, 70, 124.
    See also individual place names
University of New Brunswick, 69

Vancouver Island, 68
Vocalizations, 49, 55, 95, 105
Vosges Mountains, 9. *See also* Alsace

Weights: bobcat, 12; lynx, 19;
    mountain lion, 71
Whiskers, 29
Wild cats. *See* Cats, wild; individual
    species
Wood ghosts, 5
Wood, William, 12
Woodrat, 12, 41
World Conservation Union, 3

Yellow-bellied sapsucker, 56
Young. *See* Kittens